Candidate

Candidate

**Jerry Buttimer
with Michael Moynihan**

Gill & Macmillan

Gill & Macmillan Ltd
Hume Avenue, Park West, Dublin 12
with associated companies throughout the world
www.gillmacmillan.ie
© Jerry Buttimer 2007
978 07171 4297 2
Typography design by Make Communication
Print origination by Carrigboy Typesetting Services
Printed and bound in Great Britain by MPG Books Ltd, Bodmin, Cornwall

This book is typeset in Minion 13pt on 17pt.

All photographs are reproduced by courtesy of the *Irish Examiner.*

The paper used in this book comes from the wood pulp of managed forests. For every tree felled, at least one tree is planted, thereby renewing natural resources.

All rights reserved. No part of this publication may be copied, reproduced or transmitted in any form or by any means, without permission of the publishers.

A CIP catalogue record for this book is available from the British Library.

5 4 3 2 1

Contents

PROLOGUE 1

Diary 6

Prologue

I've been canvassing since 14 June, meaning that I'll have been at it for a year if Bertie goes to the wire. One way or the other, it will be the best part of a year. It seems months now since that midsummer day when I was joined by Michael Aherne and Bill Murphy for the first outing of the campaign.

MacCurtain Villas had the honour of being the first place canvassed. Since then we had covered Forest Ridge and Fernwood, Sandown Crescent, Lehenaghmore in Togher, Alderbrook and Seven Oaks in Douglas, Broadale estate and the Gates in Mathew Hill before June was out. The night of the intermediate hurling championship game between Bishopstown and Courcey's Rovers in Ballygarvan, we canvassed in Gleann Álainn and Gleann Dara before the game. It was a very wet night, but Bishopstown won a great game, and I hope I won a few votes as well, even when they knew I was cheering for the other side.

And so on in July through Dunvale and Parkgate estate, followed by a break in early August before covering Bellevue Estate towards the end of the month.

In September we canvassed Broadale and Willsbrook, accompanied by Derek Cregan, the son of the Cork city councillor, former senator and political legend Denis 'Dino' Cregan. In mid-September we're canvassing St Anne's Park and Derrynane Road and we mingle with supporters of Cork City on their way to the game in Turner's Cross. They're far too focused on the game to take any interest in politics. The rest of September was consumed by Mercier Park and Green Lawn, Bellevue Lawn and Close, the Ardfield estate and parts of Douglas. John, my brother, and Dad canvassed in Mahon and we also covered Deerpark.

By early October we're still finishing off the Ardfield estate, where I met a man from Co. Wexford who is a friend of my first cousin Andy in Taghmon. One of the major concerns of the residents in this estate is the traffic and the length of time it takes to get into the city each morning.

Although it's relentless, I love canvassing. So, as October wore on, it was Curragh Woods and Deerpark and Grange Heights and then on to Woodlands and Clifton Grange. There I met a man who is going to Boston for a holiday. I told him he has to go to Wrentham for shopping. This is where the big outlet stores are and where I go every summer when I visit my cousins in Boston.

In mid-October we covered Earlwood and Hillside estates, where most of the residents' concerns had to do with parking. Then, later in the month, the Uam

Var estate in Bishopstown. Then 21 October turned out to be one of the wettest days of the year. It's easy to see one resident's problems with the drain which is blocked outside his gateway and all the rain falling. We eventually decided to give in to the weather with a saturated register which we couldn't read and a notebook with the ink running down the pages.

In that same evening I attended the fiftieth anniversary dinner of the Junior Chamber of Commerce in my capacity as Deputy Lord Mayor. The minute the speeches were finished I had to dash to Bishopstown GAA, my local club, to join members of the 1976 team who were celebrating the thirtieth anniversary of winning the county championship. The following day the club were in the county final of the intermediate hurling championship against Carrigtohill. As chairman of the club, I felt just as nervous as the players and selectors. I felt a huge sense of relief and joy as the final whistle was blown and we were county champions. No canvassing that night: it was back to the clubhouse for a night of celebrations. And no canvassing the next day either: I didn't feel up to it after the night before!

Back on the trail on the 24th, however, this time it was Amberley estate and then on to Shamrock Lawn in Douglas in the succeeding days.

On 2 November, a bitterly cold night, we were in Frankfield estate in Douglas when we were joined by Mary Smithwick, political journalist with the *Evening Echo,* who was doing an article on the reaction on the doorsteps to the different candidates for her weekly column.

Since then, November has found us in Heatherton, Shrewsbury, Ballybrack, Donnybrook and Bromley Park, Hillcourt, Westgrove Lawn, Mews and Avenue, Boreenmanagh Road, parts of the Lough, Westgrove, Springbrook and Bracken Court, Carrig na Curra, Carrigaline, Wycherley Terrace and Horgan's Buildings.

It's no different for me than for anyone else, except perhaps that as a first-time candidate I have to try harder. This is all the more so given that my two party running-mates are an outgoing and a former TD. If you don't cover the ground thoroughly, meet people and listen to them, take notes and promise to do what you can about their worries and then act on that promise, you just don't get the votes. Even if you do all these things you've no guarantees, but without this kind of foot-slogging you simply have no hope at all. This is what people want in their public representatives: visibility, availability, practical action. All politics is local! Grand plans for the country's future, idealistic visions and so forth are all very commendable, but it's the hard graft on the ground that gets you votes, and nothing else.

The thing is, I love it. Like anything else, it can get you down at times, but basically I love it. I know too that people who haven't got the politics bug find it hard to understand why you'd want to put yourself through this. Well, there's one answer, weird though it may sound: I actually enjoy canvassing, walking around meeting people, shaking hands, knocking on doors. You'd want to enjoy it. If it didn't give you some sort of a kick you'd begin to start wondering about yourself.

Wednesday 22 November

Have been approached about writing a book, and meet Fergal and John to discuss it. Am I mad?

First meeting of the Estimates Committee. Joe Gavin, City Manager, announces that he proposes to increase the fee for service charges (collection of refuse) for both commercial and residential users. Many of us argue against this.

Housing is the opening directorate to be discussed, and, despite a waiting list for social and affordable housing, director Stephen Kearney gives a bravura performance, outlining plans for the year ahead. He tells us he 'got everything he wanted.' In my typical fashion I clap and congratulate Stephen on his party political broadcast on behalf of FF: you'd think there was no housing shortage, no people on lists. Some of us ask him for a video of his performance, saying it was better than Brian Cowen presenting *his* estimates.

The debate shows the FG task in the election. He's a director of services, more or less saying 'I got what I want, I can't spend any more,' yet the council has issues with waiting lists!

Evening, and rain meant we had to cancel the UCC-CIT Young FG canvass—a pity, because these guys are very committed. I go back to Bishopstown GAA club to work on the 2007 sports capital programme. As the club treasurer, Jim Collins, says, 'One thing is clear: they will dole money out and everybody will be looked after.' How right you are, Jim!

On 'Oireachtas Report' I notice that Enda Kenny has a new haircut. I had mentioned it to somebody at the presidential dinner that some people we canvassed had mentioned his hairstyle—or lack of it.

My pal David Bradley rings to tell me his mother has died. We share the experience of loss. My mother, Nancy, died on 4 August after a battle with cancer. She and Dad were the biggest influences on my life, and her words to me when I returned from Maynooth in 1990 after five years in the seminary were: 'If you think you're coming home to get involved in politics you have another think coming. Politics is a mug's game. Get a permanent job, and buy a house.'

Thursday 23 November

Opening day of the Adult Education Conference in Nenagh. No school, so I write my weekly column for the *Evening Echo*—'Bishopstown/ Wilton Notes.'

Politically the big news is that in Galway FG Councillor Brian Walsh decides to step down, leaving us with no city-based candidate. In my mind it gives Councillor Fidelma Healy-Eames a good chance; she's a very formidable person.

FF announce that the former Dublin goalie John O'Leary is to stand in Dublin North, and Michael O'Regan of the *Irish Times* on the 'News at One' gives him an outstanding chance. Mairéad McGuinness is mentioned for Louth; now there's a good one. Fergus O'Dowd is one of the good performers in the Dáil, and there's no hope of a second seat in Louth in my view. Keep Mairéad in Europe. What is it about all the MEPs wanting to come home?

No canvassing today, and I'm getting withdrawal symptoms, with no knocking on doors or talking to people and debating. The Lord Mayor, Councillor Michael Aherne, says repeatedly, the more people you meet the better you'll do.

In Nenagh I met Michael Lowry TD briefly in the hotel lobby. He looks pale. I remember him in the Hugh Coveney by-election in 1994; he was an impressive organiser who demanded action and results. The morning of the poll, after a late, late night, the constituency office in Cook Street was locked and Lowry booted it in, saying, 'We've work to do; there's nothing won yet.' I wonder what he would have been like as leader of FG.

Can't delay at Nenagh, have to get back to Cork for a constituency meeting in Carrigaline Court Hotel, and I interrupt Jim O'Keeffe in the middle of a speech. He gives a passionate speech about the need for the party to hold its nerve, but Deirdre Clune says maybe we will only win one seat!

I'm full of life, urging people on and heaping criticism on SF.

Friday 24 November

Wet, wild and windy. In Belfast Michael Stone crashes the party as Ian Paisley stops short of saying he'll accept the post of First Minister. Typical DUP fudge. I agree with the Taoiseach: 'It's time for clarity in Northern Ireland.'

The TV footage of Stone shows the craziness that exists on both sides, and the old they-haven't-gone-away adage resonates.

Gay Mitchell shocks us by announcing his decision not to contest Dublin South-Central. Is his decision to stay in Europe an omen that power is slipping away? This makes Dublin more difficult. I wonder about the option of Catherine Byrne and/or one of the Mitchell girls. To me Gay is an icon, a trojan worker, a vociferous debater and a true TV performer.

Tonight's our fund-raiser event in Bishopstown GAA club. Ticket sales going okay—I hate selling tickets, it's a worry if few turn up. Before that another pre-budget meeting in City Hall.

In the end the fund-raiser's a good night, swapping stories, meeting friends. Great support from party membership, GAA people and friends. Simon Coveney arrives late and Derek T. asks repeatedly if he paid his €20. Simon smiles, says he must; later, as he prepares to leave, Derek roars across the function room not to forget to pay his €20. Simon smiles and leaves.

Saturday 25 November

Canvass Ballyphehane 12–4 p.m., but Saturday mornings begin with tea in the Bishopstown GAA club. It's a good way to meet people, get a feel for where they're at.

In Ballyphehane it's Rita, Mossie, Dad, Michael Aherne and me. We start in MacDonagh Road, sun shining, but it's slow to start, with people out shopping on Saturday morning. Respect for the elderly is raised, ball-playing on the green, law and order: 'Need to change the Government; sure I know a fella was sentenced Monday and out Tuesday. We have people doing well selling drugs and what happens? Nothing. I hope you get in.'

Feeling upbeat, but Rita's urging us to move on ('You're too long at that door . . .'). What can you do? As a new candidate I feel I have to take my time at the doors.

One woman mentions young people: 'There are no facilities for young people in the area. Where are they going to go on a winter's evening?' I agree: maybe in the council's leisure and recreation SPC we could raise the issue. Young people on street corners, drinking and engaging in vandalism is an issue raised in all estates, but it's always a small minority involved.

Moving along Plunkett Road and Sarahville, Councillor and former Senator Denis 'Dino' Cregan's name is constantly mentioned: 'Oh, is Dino not running? He's my man.' No, he's not, I say, adding that he calls me his eighth child.

The afternoon is better, with more people at home. At one door an elderly gent says: 'Ah, the Bishopstown man; you're having a great year, ye'll be taking over from the Barrs.'

I say: 'If we do half as well up senior as ye did we'll be all right.'

'Go on away, I'll look after you. It'll be my first time voting FG, but we need a change.'

We finish off when Dad meets an old friend. They reminisce, and memories of Mum come flooding back. She would have loved the buzz of campaigning. I smile and cry on the way to the car, thinking of what she said in the local elections: 'The ballot box is a great leveller.'

Sunday 26 November

Munster club semi-final, Bishopstown v. Claughaun. Politically the day's dominated by two polls. The *Sunday Business Post* poll: FG no change, and headline says FF retains lead over FG and Labour.

Off to Blackrock for church gate collection. Constituency secretary Laura is in poor form, upset by polls. 'What do we have to do?' she says.

Lady and daughter approach. When they see the collection box the girl says: 'FG collectors? No way. You need no money . . .'

The mother's dropped money into the box before realising and agrees with daughter: 'FG? God help us, you're down in the polls, going nowhere; Bertie is the man.'

Maybe she's right, but I don't think so. It's all about the need to keep hope, though Hillary Clinton's words come back to me: hope is not a strategy for success.

The second opinion poll, on TG4, is another morale-sapper: FG gain in South Kerry is unlikely. It's ten days to the budget, and at the end of a week of two killings and serious assaults FF are still looking strong.

Crime continues to be raised as a serious issue, yet the media ridicule the boot camp suggestion of Billy Timmins. More needs to be done to tackle low-level, annoying anti-social behaviour. Enda Kenny said in the Dáil that Ireland's like a 21st-century Dodge City. Laws may be there, but crime and killing continue.

Minister Mícheál Martin and his entourage were out in force at the Masses on Curraheen Road in Bishopstown, which got me a huge slagging at the Munster club semi-final.

Elsewhere, Mildred Fox will not stand again in Wicklow. Time will tell if Andrew Doyle can take advantage there for FG.

Sat down with John and Rita to review the week. Weather so bad we had only a few nights' canvass. Planning is important, so we decide to head for Ballyphehane again next Sunday. In publicity, we agree to raise the issue of extension of voter registration, the dyslexia case, and local issues.

Feel down, but members call, including Kevin McGarry: 'Are these polls true? Jesus, they can't be. Sure the people are roaring at us for change. Aren't they?' Kevin and his wife Noreen are Trojan workers for the Party, who tirelessly give their time.

Monday 27 November

FG UCC strategy committee meeting; John and Noel attend. Meeting agrees to a series of 'town hall meetings' with candidates at several locations around the constituency and the need for candidates to submit their canvass schedule.

Deirdre Clune, according to Fidelma Collins, is out Tuesday and Saturday, Simon Coveney on Saturday only. Me? As often as I can.

Day dominated by meetings. CASP meeting in County Hall is effectively run by Tomas Ryan. I raise the issue of the two flyovers at SWC Road and Bandon Road and the need for a traffic plan for Douglas.

Second meeting is at the Shandon Court Hotel with the home help organisation. They have issues with their hours being cut, privatisation and/or means-testing for the medical card. Another big issue in this election.

Tuesday 28 November

The big news today is the draft EU report into alleged CIA rendition flights, which expresses 'serious concerns' over the 147 US stopovers in Shannon.

I get a call from a gent concerned about his safety. 'My house is in the flight path of Cork Airport,' he says. 'George Bush won't be here to save me.'

'No, he won't,' I say. 'But I think you'll agree that Cork Airport has no CIA-operated flights.'

'Jerry, what happens if there's fog in Shannon? Farranfore is too small.'

'Okay, I'll raise it with our spokesman on foreign affairs.'

The other big story is the publication of the OECD report which forecasts a 5 per cent growth in the Irish economy—but there's a catch: in 2008 it's to be 4.5 per cent. Is there going to be a slowdown just as we're on the verge of government? The OECD warns that 'boosting competition in the electricity and gas sectors was becoming a matter of urgency.' Indeed; ask the voters who are outraged at the upward spiral of energy costs.

Afternoon: Navigation House on Albert Quay is Cork City Council's planning department. This afternoon we're discussing the Bishopstown-Wilton Area Action Plan.

Wednesday 29 November

Canvassing in the afternoon with Bill Murphy and Michael Aherne. Bill, chairperson of the Michael Collins Branch, selects Horgan's Buildings in the Cork North-West Ward of College View. It's a small row of semi-detached houses adjacent to UCC.

Typically, the issue of noise from students is raised: 'Do they have any consideration for us? It used to be just Thursday night, now it's almost every night. And come here, we won't mention the carry-on of them.'

Bill interjects to inform that I too attended UCC. I reply that I often was that student who probably enjoyed the crack on College Road late at night after a night out.

Issues of road-cleaning and clearing away leaves are also raised. Thankfully, I'd just placed a motion before the council calling on the environment directorate to come up with a new strategy for on-street parking. Still, in 2006 it's hard to explain why, in an economy as rich as Ireland's, people are afraid. But they are. Time and again today the question of public lighting is raised. One lady says matter-of-factly: 'I don't feel safe walking at night, and I shouldn't have to feel that way.' No, you shouldn't.

Bill—again good to have the local knowledge—informs her that the community garda is available to talk to. I agree to check with Cork City Council and the ESB to see if we can improve the situation.

Michael Aherne, another party loyalist, joins us as the rain threatens. The banter ignites; Michael, always a ball-hopper, tells me that John Dennehy of FF was in Glendale East canvassing last Saturday, and that all my work is in vain, as John will take care of it.

Ellen Condon, 90 in February, answers the door with a smile: 'Hello, boy, you're my crowd. Mr Murphy always brings me down to vote.'

I assure her I won't forget her.

'Good,' she says. 'I've voted all my life; it's my duty, and sure wouldn't it be great to have you in the Dáil.'

I smile, agree, and feel it's worth while to be out on this cold day.

'I hope to make the hundred,' she says. 'The cheque from the President would come in handy.'

Not surprisingly on a cold November day, many of the elderly residents complain about the high cost of gas bills ('€160 for two months, €95 ESB—it's hard to keep warm.')

We meet a lady of 94, full of the joys of life. When I ask if she has any queries she says: 'Just one, really. I'm praying that our Holy Father will come home safely from Turkey. Do you think he'll get home safe?' Yes, I say. Pray for him, she says; I tell her I spent five years in Maynooth.

Later we disturb a lady trying to get cat hair out of the carpet. 'Fine Gael? No way; but I always voted for Liam Burke, he was so good to me. If you're half as good as him you'll be fine. But tell Enda Kenny he's like Woody in *Toy Story*. He has two movements: his elbow goes up and down.'

Next door no better. 'We know what the Government are doing: nothing. We never hear of what FG are going to. Them fellas on the telly, it's like a slagging match, they never listen. And while you're at it you can double Bertie's make-up bill, God help him, he needs it.'

A lot of the houses are rented out, with the tenants keeping their votes at home. One man reminds us that the Premiership is on the telly: 'You'll lose a lot of votes if you call and they miss a goal.'

We finish off by calling to John Quirke, Cork North-Central FG constituency chairman. 'You're the first FG general election candidate to call to my house.' A good way to end the night.

Thursday 30 November

Rain, rain, go away. I love canvassing, despite my protests, but Rita, John, Dad and I agree to postpone tonight's canvass because of the incessant rain. We have a brief chat on where we stand: canvass 70 per cent of Grange-Frankfield; dropped all of local ward with the South-West Ward newsletter; letters: issued 425 in November.

Rita is my left and right arm. She's the person who keeps me on track, volunteering on a nightly basis to type and canvass, along with being a good friend.

We spend the evening in the office upstairs in my house going through correspondence—even more to do. Every evening after canvassing Rita collates the queries and notes from each area. She opens a file in the computer—and in the filing cabinet. Every query receives a name, and letters are sent—we prefer the old way. It's a matter of debate between us, but Rita prefers letters, and she, as normal, wins!

Politically the news is dominated by the publication of a Dáil committee report proposing to lower the age of consent to sixteen. Fiona Neary of the Rape Crisis Centre is on the 'News at One', very strong remarks, saying it was wrong to lower the age from seventeen. Enda Kenny says the recommendation on the legal age of consent sends the wrong signals to children and society.

Séamus Brennan is on the news, saying next week's budget will increase the state pension to at least €200 per week: 'I can confirm that we will at least meet that target. What we can do ahead of that remains to be seen in the next week.' Indeed.

Deirdre Clune hosts a breakfast fund-raiser in the Millennium Hall in City Hall, €50 a head. Phil Hogan TD is guest speaker. He's a good warm-up act at the ard-fheis, and this morning he opens with the usual smart comments, special greetings from one man in Kilkenny, Liam McCarthy.

Yeah, Phil, it still hurts, the loss of three in a row.

Friday 1 December

Will this weather ever clear? It's been rain since I started this diary, but I keep saying 'more canvassing,' as it's the one thing I love about politics.

The first time I went canvassing was in the local elections of 1979. I followed my dad along Bishopstown as he canvassed for Bram Bermingham in the local elections. I remember being caught by Dad, who wanted me to go home, but another canvasser said I could carry the leaflets and stay out by the gates as he went in. I loved it.

I remember waiting in for Garret's European bus in Dunne's Stores and shaking hands with Alan Dukes and Jim O'Keeffe and John Blair, our European candidates. I called Jim O'Keeffe by John Blair's name. Little did I think that twenty-seven years later we would both be running for FG in a general election.

Today's very hard. A chest infection, and it's Mum's first birthday since she died. She was the best politician never elected. She had a word for everyone; she could talk for Ireland, and she always said, 'Treat everybody the same.' One of the few days she cried during her illness was when Enda Kenny came to visit her in the Bon Secours. It meant so much to her to have him sit in the hospital chair and joke with her.

Today is about meetings. Residents opposed to the proposed redevelopment of Musgrave Park, then a second meeting closer to home, the Woodbrook Residents' Association. The late Liam Burke advised me when elected, whatever else you do go to your residents' meetings: they're the people who elected you.

Saturday 2 December

Canvass 12–4, Ballyphehane. Cold, blustery day. Meet Mossie Phelan, John Stanton, Noel Cregan and Rita, and we do Botanic Road and Kent Road.

We're well organised—register, notebooks, pens— and away we go. Overhead the sky's black, but we're determined. Mossie is a lone voice in the parish running the FG show. Responses vary: 'That energy regulator is a licence to print money for the Government.'

'Politician? No, boy, you're all corrupt. You may not be now, but after three weeks in there they'll sort you out.'

Schools having to pay waste collection and rates is one issue raised, but the crack is good and we're all enjoying the banter even when Mrs Barry tells me she votes FF but I might get her number 4. Her son Father Pat played for Cork in 1976, winning an All-Ireland hurling medal.

Many of the residents are concerned with the high cost of their gas bills and with the slowness of the ESB repairing public lighting.

It's raining hard so we take shelter in the alley to the side of one of the houses, and Mossie gives us an impromptu lesson on the history of Ballyphehane. The rain stops and we head off. Progress is mixed. Many gone out shopping or putting up the Christmas decorations.

Again we're told: 'You're all tarred with the one brush, only work a few days a week and ye get lots of money and a great pension. What do we get? Pay up and look pleasant.'

I meet a past pupil of mine, Bernard Considine, and his new baby, Ellen, just three weeks old. We politicians will do anything for a vote.

Then comes a heated debate with a SF supporter who is so anti-FG. When I tell that I am a republican, nationalist and in favour of a 32-county Ireland by consent, not by bullet, he lets me have it: 'Gerry Adams and Martin McGuinness would not have got to the negotiation table without the IRA campaign.'

No, I say, they were not right.

'What about Mrs Thatcher?'

It's time to leave, because I believe in a 32-county Ireland and want to see a united Ireland and an end to British rule but not through violence.

Another voter gives me advice for Enda ('Tell him to be a bit louder'). I promise to pass it on.

What is it about Enda? To me he's an excellent leader, intelligent, witty, ordinary and genuinely caring. Why can't this be communicated more effectively?

It's heading for 3:45 as we finish—because of the rain.

Sunday 3 December

Sunday ahead of the budget. Trouble in Galway West. *Sunday Independent* headline: 'Kenny's plea to TD causes FG turmoil.'

Following on from Brian Walsh's decision not to run, Pádraic McCormack is coming under pressure from Enda Kenny to reconsider. This has incurred the wrath of Fidelma Healy-Eames. It's a hard one to call, whether one should come out of retirement or not. Pádraic McCormack is a very dedicated constituency worker. This is a very delicate and sensitive matter. I just hope that we get it right. It's about winning a seat and if possible two.

Radio is all about the budget. Brian Cowen must be happy. It's an extraordinary position to be in, with so much surplus money to spend, save or give back to the people. Of course, it's the taxpayers' money in the first place.

The pre-budget forecasts were €4.86 billion, with the newspapers telling us the surplus money is close to €46 million and that Brian Cowen will cut stamp duty, reduce tax and look after the elderly.

'The Week in Politics' has thirty swing or floating voters with the American pollster Frank Luntz. The floating voters are from the commuter belt area around Dublin. These are the swing voters, the undecided, the people who will either vote for change or vote for the status quo. It reminds me of a comment from a FG canvasser: 'Who are these mystical people, the floating voters?'

It seems all of us are playing for a 25–20 per cent voter segment of the electorate.

When asked to say how Ireland is viewed nowadays, those polled say: 'Changed, better but more difficult, warm but difficult, stressful, good for some, not for others.'

As I was watching the programme I thought the image of Bertie was too visible, too prominent. Something we have to do in the new year is to organise those town hall meetings with residents, a meet and greet.

Health emerges as the number 1 issue—hardly surprising, as every night we're regaled by stories of A&E queues.

The focus groups call Bertie decent and personable, a man of the people, hardworking—but not accountable. It's interesting how FF have cultivated Bertie the man. One night a young voter told us he's voting 'because of Gift Grub; it's just class, you have to vote for the Bert.'

Enda Kenny gets a lashing on the programme, it's unfair in my mind: 'Lacks punch, not strong enough, no charisma, no bottle, boring and dull, does what he's told.' To me it's not making sense: look at the way he organised FG since the 2002 debacle; the man is charismatic and not dull, he's personable, ordinary, down to earth; if he did what he's told we'd be worse now than we were in 2002.

The overriding impression is that the party is doing okay with the wrong leader. Bullshit: Enda is my man. He will be a good Taoiseach; as Ivan Yates said, 'The job makes the man.' John Bruton had 10 per cent approval in October '94 and was up to 58 per cent in January '95.

McDowell got savaged—intelligent, boring and arrogant. Rabbitte had a 50 per cent favourable rating, but the preferred Government option is FF and Labour. So, where to now? The old Bill Clinton comment: 'It's the economy, stupid.'

There's a clear need for better delivery of services and for accountability with public money.

Enda Kenny's comment in one of his first speeches at a party gathering comes to mind: 'It's in your hands' —literally, with the FG members to go and fight for every vote and for the swing voter to give us a chance.

Monday 4 December

City council meeting day. A meeting of the Roads Function Committee is preceded by the Roads Strategic Policy Committee. We have a motion before the committee calling on the city council to review its policy of clamping, with a view to ending the policy.

Dan Buggy is the assistant city manger in charge of roads and transport, and he comes with a tough reputation, but I've found him to be a man to get things done.

Clamping is a contentious issue that's drawing the ire of people: just a month ago I had to plead with a constituent to get out of of his car and to allow the clampers to take the vehicle away. He was sitting in his vehicle on top of the tow truck—with gardaí in attendance.

It was agreed to review the policy and its operation in 2007.

I also attended a meeting of the Passage-Monkstown Fine Gael branch. Rain is falling heavily—canvassing is again cancelled, but the meeting is a good, lively one, spent discussing the polls and 'The Week in Politics'. Deirdre Clune repeats her comments that FG can only win one seat.

The weather has dominated people's minds, with obvious damage caused by floods across the country. Crossmolina was badly hit, but locally the Lee Road was closed and part of Carrigrohane Road was flooded. It prompted Tomas Ryan to slag me: 'If you guys in the City Hall want a boundary extension ye'd better handle the flooding better . . .'

Tuesday 5 December

It's the eve of the budget, and, as in 2005, a junior minister threatens to hijack Brian Cowen's speech: in a controversial interview on 'Prime Time Investigates' Minister Tim O'Malley makes a gaff about waiting lists. Bertie didn't exactly come to his junior minister's defence, saying: 'Mr O'Malley was doing the job to the best of his ability.' The programme highlighted HSE issues regarding waiting lists in the mental health area: 3,000 children under sixteen are on waiting lists just to get a diagnosis; where a child lives determines how long they'll be on the list, while the programme claimed that almost one-third of children suffer from a serious dysfunctional disorder.

Strategy meeting in the afternoon, our first in a while. We agree a formula of publication of material: one A4 newsletter covering the hot-button issues—health, housing, education, value for money—and 10,000 leaflets to be issued in February in Grange and north-west area.

We agree to canvass up to Friday the 15th, before breaking up for Christmas.

Wednesday 6 December

Budget day, afternoon. Canvass with Michael Aherne and Bill Murphy. The dry, sunny morning has given way to an overcast afternoon with rain looming.

Here we are—what a contrast to Brian Cowen. Well-respected minister, a shoo-in for re-election and about to read his third budget; me, rookie general election candidate, two-and-a-half years on Cork City Council, out on a dour December afternoon, knocking on doors.

Jeez, is it worth it? Does every candidate feel the same? Little acorns, big oak trees. I think of Barack Obama in the USA—could he and I make it?

Pádraic McCormack has reconsidered his decision to retire and will run again in Galway West. Fidelma Healy-Eames is very vocal on radio—comes across as articulate and confident.

Our afternoon canvass is very close to UCC—hard to believe that the college dominates an area so much.

'You're the first candidate to call in my twelve years here.'

'That must be worth something,' I say.

'It might be.'

In the shop we meet some UCC students, and we engage in conversation—one is studying geography and Irish: 'I'm not sure I like it but the crack is good.'

Student 2 says about voting: 'I'll do what my parents say.'

The issues start to arise among other residents when we knock on doors—students parking without discs ('If you didn't close the gate they'd nearly park inside in the house').

The budget is raised: 'I hope they look after us widows. Ye're not doing much for us—we have to pay for everything—refuse, TV. If I work I have to pay tax . . . Not to mention Joe Gavin: if he gets his way we'll have to pay for the bins too.'

The usual litany: speed on the roads, parking, students making noise.

Two students answer the door at another house—one has no interest but the other's on the phone: 'Mum, it's a Fine Gael candidate.' I'm given the phone and the mother says she's supporting Andrew Doyle in Wicklow. 'Good, keep it up.'

Another house, and a student from west Cork. 'I'm not changing my vote, I'm keeping it in west Cork.'

Why?

'I'm voting for change; I'm voting for P. J. Sheehan, he'll get the job done.'

We move down to Highfield Avenue—rented houses, mostly. The long-time residents are vocal: 'We're paying for thirty years of bad planning. Look at the paths, the roads are the same as twenty-five years ago . . . This area's been decimated, it's now a wasteland of student accommodation. The college have been allowed to build with no thought for the residents, no proper parking, and all we get is "we need to have higher density".

Then there're the students.

Me: 'Hi, have you voted before?'
Girl: 'I did, in the European Elections in 2004.'
Me: 'For who?'
Girl: 'Simon Coveney, he's so handsome.'
Me: 'He is.'
Girl: 'You're not Simon Coveney.'
Me: 'No, I'm not.' No argument there.

That night the AGM of Bishopstown GAA club. It's the heartbeat of our community, it's what gives meaning to Bishopstown. I'm proud to be elected chairman again. For a fifth—and final—time.

Thursday 7 December

Eagle Valley is one of the housing estates on the edge of Cork city, opened to cater for CUH, CIT and FÁS, rented out in the main. The evening sky's covered in dark clouds, but we set out to canvass.

From house 9 to 102 not a single registered voter. None interested in transferring their vote from Clare, Kerry, Tipperary, Waterford, west Cork, Poland or Pakistan.

('Nah, voting for Jackie Healy-Rae, he got my mother's road tarred.' 'My Dad would kill me if I didn't go home to vote—life isn't worth that.')

The Pakistani works in a city hospital. 'There's a communications gap between the hospital consultant and the local GP, but I like your health system.' Glad someone thinks so.

Many people look at us with a jaundiced eye: 'Ye're out early . . . is there an election?'

Do we keep going? Rita says yes, it'll be worth it.

One image stays with me, though: a group of Poles playing cards in the front room of a house; new immigrants, on a cold, wet night, gathered together. They open the door gingerly.

'I don't speak much English . . . Can I vote?'

'Yes, for local and European elections.'

'Oh, not for parliament. Okay, thanks for calling.'

Olwyn Enright's proposal to lengthen the school year draws the ire of a teacher. 'Seven thousand teachers will hammer you. Does she have a clue? And remember, we all vote, and so do our partners.'

No argument from me. I love June, July and August.

The final house of the evening, as the cold bites and the rain falls—a complaint about the traffic, sequencing of traffic lights: 'Are engineers and project managers human or do they live on another planet?' I agree dutifully.

Politically the day after the budget is dominated by reaction to the 'good news', but the European Central Bank threw a spanner in the works by raising interest rates by 0.25 per cent, 24 hours after Brian Cowen announced the doubling of mortgage relief for first-time home-buyers. That's six interest rate rises in twelve months.

Friday 8 December

The feast of the Immaculate Conception. Once the start of the Christmas shopping, now just a blip on the screen. No longer the country day out in town either.

Canvassing the Mardyke tonight. I can't get over how shook the area has become: the Mardyke Arena has blotted out the view of part of Sunday's Well.

The first greeting at a door: 'The Mardyke needs renovation and regeneration.'

No doubt that the UCC sports centre is a fine facility but it's caused turmoil for the residents and has changed the topography of the Dyke. Another lady is ready, waiting at the door, saying parking is bad from 10 a.m. to 5 p.m. She says because of cars and heavy vehicles she's denied access to her house. 'And what do I get from politicians and the council? —silence. The neglect of residents in the Mardyke is unbelievable.'

Walking the area, it's clear that many of the houses are let out and have lost their former glories. For those still living in the area it's a crying shame.

I have to admit that at the time of the building of the arena I didn't comprehend the views of residents, being a proud UCC man who, while a student campaigner, campaigned for a new sports facility—and wanted it at any cost. Now as a politician I see the arena has brewed up a storm.

As the rain falls—again—we continue to debate with residents about local issues: parking, the state of the roads, clamping. Mrs Cantwell: 'I've no interest in people running for elections who don't take an interest in us.'

As we finish the canvass there's been no mention of the budget or Bertie. The message is clear: regenerate the Mardyke. City Hall provides the final backdrop to the day as the Lord Mayor hosts a reception for the Cork camogie and women's football teams.

Saturday 9 December

'Tis the season to be jolly? Young FG are out on the campaign trail, some of whom haven't canvassed before. We're pencilled in for Farranlea Grove and Park on Model Farm Road. It's part of

Cork North-West Ward, represented by Colm Burke. Colm's one of the most genuine people I've encountered in FG: he always looks at the bigger picture, what's best for the party.

The canvass begins at 11:50 a.m. and flooding, again, is a big concern. One resident asks us what the plans are for the flood relief in the Lee Road and the Carrigrohane Straight. We talk about the effect of the dam releasing water and all agree the staff are excellent there.

The pace continues, with Catrina Burke driving us on. Morning is dry, the YFG members are enjoying themselves, buoyed by the praise heaped on Colm Burke, the local man. The budget is raised at a number of doors: 'This is a cod; they give us something, but we've to pay tax, and prices have gone up. Do they take us for fools?'

'Come on, I've never had it so good. FF are the boys—look at my pension!' No point arguing with that; thanks for your time.

It's the usual mix: need for traffic calming, parking, rented properties, high-rise apartments. We break at 2:15, off to the Rendezvous bar. Just as we resume in the afternoon I get an anonymous text: 'Welcome to CSD country, Jerry Buttimer.' (CSD is Communities for Sustainable Development.)

I reply: 'I think you're mixed up. I'm in Model Farm Road, but thanks for the welcome.'

Another text in reply: 'You're the one who's mixed up, it's CSD country but thanks for calling.'

The afternoon is slower. 'Bishopstown has been left behind, we have no village, no shop, no post office, no social services, no public paths. The planners have let us down.'

Tip O'Neill said all politics is local. He was right.

As we finish, a lovely lady brings me into her house to show the encroachment of apartment complexes all around her and the effect that has on her privacy. 'I'm thinking of selling,' she says.

'Don't move,' I reply.

'I'll be a rich corpse here,' she says. 'What good will that be to me?'

Sunday 10 December

It's meant to be the Munster intermediate club hurling final today but the weather plays spoilsport. Luckily we were only on the bus in Bishopstown when the news came through. So what to do now?

We look at the weekly plan. Monday: 3:30 p.m., FG meeting. 4 p.m., roads sec. 4:30 p.m., FG councillors' meeting. 5:30 p.m., council meeting. 8 p.m., Fernwood residents. 9 p.m., Bishopstown GAA Club executive meeting.

Tuesday: 4 p.m., sports committee. 5:30 p.m., Recreation SPC. 7 p.m., Leisureworld meeting. 8:30 p.m., dinner.

Wednesday: 10:30 a.m., City Development Board. 3–4:30 p.m., senior citizens' party. 8 p.m., YFG Christmas party.

Thursday: 11 a.m. HSE subcommittee (Kilkenny). 6:45 p.m., minor replay, Páirc Uí Chaoimh. 8 p.m., Deputy Lord Mayor, Gaelscoil Uí Riada.

'When are we going to canvass?' I'm asked. 'After midnight or before 9 a.m.,' I reply.

We agree to two afternoon canvasses, on Tuesday and Wednesday. It's getting near Christmas and people won't want the hassle.

Don't forget there's school, GAA, letters and e-mails to be sent and replied to, not to mention phone calls. Who said being a politician was easy? I enjoy the buzz, though it's a full-time activity. I find it difficult as a single person to manage my time, I can only imagine what it's like being a full-time politician with a young family.

Sunday 17 December

One Sunday newspaper headline chillingly grabs my attention: 'The killing streets: Now they are shooting the innocent.' The number of people since the start of 2006 who have lost their lives in a violent death stands at sixty-five, an increase of two since last year.

Is this the same Government who nine years ago promised zero tolerance, who berated Nora Owen at every opportunity? BUPA Ireland take out a full-page advert in the papers, telling us why they have 'closed for business . . . We would be required over the next 3 years, to pay €161 million in risk payments to our competitor the dominant market insurer . . .'

The Sunday before Christmas (next one is Christmas Eve) and Cork city is busy, restaurants full. A moment to catch oneself comes on Union Quay, where a number of girls from Innishannon are putting notices on car windscreens.

I ask: 'What are you littering us with now?' thinking foolishly that it's a promotional leaflet.

'We're looking for information on our friend who's been missing since Thursday.'

It's an extraordinary moment: here is Cork buzzing with excitement but a group of students who should be enjoying the build-up to Christmas are out seeking their friend.

Life is precious—a gift that many of us don't appreciate. Being a public representative has taken me into many people's homes. You get to see people in need, the elderly afraid to open the door. Some looking forward to a visitor, others just want to chat. It's an Ireland that is becoming more political: those who have, those who have not, those who want.

This year no cards in our house, no sense of Christmas. One major force and presence in the family's life is missing. My mum.

'The Week in Politics' is usual fare on a Sunday night for political junkies, this week no exception. Festive spice added by the presence of Mairéad McGuinness. Will she run or will she not? is the burning question. Gay Mitchell, Jim Higgins, Avril Doyle all remaining in Europe, while Simon Coveney declared early on his desire to return, but Mairéad still ponders, hands out, telling Seán O'Rourke: 'I'll text you ...'

This morning after Mass I met a Fine Gael supporter who was full of joy: 'It's just eight months to the Rainbow.'

Monday 18 December

A week to Christmas, the last week of school term. Staff and students are feeling tired. Exams are on and it's estimates day in City Hall.

Over the weekend a number of us FG councillors chat on the phone. We have huge reservations about the €3 fee per lift on the bin charges proposed by the City Manager, but I love the work of being a councillor. There hasn't been a day since being elected that I haven't enjoyed it. Walking in the door of City Hall and sitting in the council chamber as a member of Cork City Council is an honour, a privilege and humbling.

First meeting with the IRFU regarding the development of Musgrave Park. Naturally the IRFU want to build a new stand, upgrade Musgrave Park and attract Munster games to Cork. Some local residents are upset and angry at the plans. The IRFU inform us that Limerick is building its city around Munster; are we seriously suggesting that Thomond Park would be replaced as the home of rugby in Munster? I don't think so. The part I have a problem with is the proposal to sell off 'ancillary land' and with it the use of sporting grounds.

Meeting of CPG. The manager informs us that this a.m. he received €1 million from the Government. Just like that. Magic.

With the question of the service charge issue defused, the councillors' meeting looks at other parts of the budget. Overall it seems fair, with many projects being brought to fruition.

Council meeting is at 5:30—protocol dictates that the city manager accompanies the Lord Mayor into the chamber, where we all stand up. It's heading to an anti-climax but Councillor Chris O'Leary, a good man for the dramatics, proposes an adjournment for a few weeks so that in the light of the manager's declaration of new money received we can study the budget. I am happy to support him, as is Seán Martin. I know that it won't win but still feel he has a point.

Pat the Protester, as he is known in Cork, disrupts the meeting; he's dressed as Santa and bursts in the door of the council chamber, demanding a cut in service charges. The Lord Mayor rings the bell to suspend the meeting, at which point Seán Martin and I get up to walk out. I seriously thought of tackling him but on seeing who it was I smiled and walked out.

Only in Cork could a fellow like Pat end up in the tea room having a cup of tea in the company of a few of us. 'I've been protesting for thirty-seven years,' he says. 'It's my right.'

At 7:15 all of us head into the Lord Mayor's chamber for a festive drink. Denis O'Flynn, the Labour councillor for South-East Ward, was pulling pints. They looked good.

Tuesday 19 December

In schools across the country thousands of students are in exam halls facing Christmas tests. Supervision is dreary but worth while.

In the middle of the morning break I receive an excited phone call from a neighbour in Bishopstown. 'In the middle of dinner last night I received a call from a marketing company asking me to take part in a marketing survey.—No, I don't do them, but when he said it was one to do with the general election I thought of you. He asked me under which category would you think is the most important: health, child care, crime, jobs, transport. I picked health and child care. Then he asked me to select the person I would vote for and he called out the names: Boyle, Buttimer, Clune, Coveney. I stopped him and said Buttimer. I was then asked why. I replied: in touch with constituents, hard-working, always available, couldn't be more helpful.'

Thanks, I reply, curious as to who was carrying out the poll in Christmas week. Perhaps it was another bogus poll, but nonetheless it created interest and makes you realise that polls do paint a picture. They do create a momentum and portray a candidate as the one to back. Labour in the week after the '92 election built a momentum, while a series of polls created a mood within Fine Gael to oust John Bruton. Today he comes into my mind a lot. Why, I've no idea, but to me he was a leader. I didn't agree with him on Northern Ireland, but he was no John Unionist.

The interim Moriarty Tribunal findings are published. There's a need for balance in developing places —I've opposed developments in my own city because I feel they are contrary to good planning. I accept that developers have needs and on occasion I have objected to some proposals because of electoral pressure. There is a need for balance. Sometimes this is difficult to achieve.

But developers equally in my mind don't get the full picture. They see money as their means. As I travel around Dublin I see parts of Dublin West and Dublin Mid-West, Palmerstown, Lucan, Blanchardstown, and in Cork on the edge of the city in Grange, Douglas, Donnybrook, becoming suburbia of housing, commercial retail, and little or no green area. Very few public amenities. So is this what we want?

22 December 2006 to 4 January 2007

The death of Mr Justice Seán O'Leary on 22 December; a council meeting early morning and then off to the Mass and burial. It was a Fine Gael occasion. Seán was one of those figures whom we looked up to. He was the definitive word on figures, who would win and lose. To my generation he was more than one of Garret's handlers: he was a man of conviction, a man who was a true Fine Gaeler, a former lord mayor, councillor, senator and judge. John Bruton described Seán brilliantly: 'A deeply humane and loveable person who held the most prominent and varied positions in public life, without ever losing his humility or his brilliant sense of humour.'

We have taken a decision to end canvassing and politicking until early January—something I hate, but promise to renew with vigour my determination to win a seat in the new year.

Christmas is a time when we all hope to switch off. It's an opportunity to recharge and to let your body slow down and rest. I am amazed at the volume of work local politicians carry out on a part-time basis. So many people think we are full-time and forget that we aren't, or that a vast number have to hold down a job.

Christmas shopping in Cork is always fun, especially for me, as the Christmas season is the happiest time of the year. Two of my nieces, Éabha and Sinéad, are so excited about Santa that they have asked us all to go to bed early. Anthony Dennehy in a Christmas Day text asks, 'Is he making you wait till May for one of his presents?' I hope so. I promise to be good, Santa, to canvass all the time and to work diligently for the people!

Retired judge Fergus Flood started the holiday period off when he criticised the Minister for Justice, Michael McDowell, over his remarks about the failure of judges to implement the law on bail and mandatory sentences for drug-dealing. Classical silly season, and this was added to by the seeming boycott of the minister's drinks reception for them.

Christmas 2006 is different; it's the first without Mum, and her void is huge. Like every home without a mother, it's emotional, and for us all the absence of her is hard to take. The visit to the grave on Christmas Day and New Year's Day was not easy. The outpouring of emotion by each of us helps and we all feel for Dad. At Mass on Christmas Day I keep thinking of Mum's words to me: 'Treat everybody the same.'

Thursday 4 January

First night of canvassing of new year and we head to Togher and the rural part of the constituency. It's probably going to be a good area for John Dennehy, the local TD. People are either home from work or back from the sales. Even though Christmas is not over we—or maybe I—feel the need to go out and knock on doors. It's cold and dark but the normal chill of early January is missing.

It's a very quiet canvass, just Rita and me, as we meet many at home. It was fun to canvass homes with Christmas decorations, lights on in the windows and trees lighting. Offers of cake and sweets were plentiful but alas no time to sit and drink tea. The whole issue of care of our elderly, local services like grass-cutting, road repairs were all raised and, as usual, the need for change.

'If you don't win this year's general election you failed, and I'll be looking for your job'—the sentence that sent FG into the headlines. John Deasy in a radio interview ignited a debate that none of us want and that has riddled the party for decades: the leadership. I am an Enda Kenny supporter, always have been and believe that he is doing a good job.

The debate continued when Councillor John Carey got in on the act. Now I have to admit I'm fond of both guys, and John Carey is a likeable character. Carey said John Deasy is 'an ambitious politician supporting Enda up to general election and I believe that after that there should be a leadership challenge. There is nothing new in that.'

Gavin Jennings asks: 'A divided family once again; why can't we keep united?' Good question, but it's all of us rowing in the one direction and raising the profile of the party. Enda lost a lot of ground in the way he handled Bertie Ahern's money issue.

This is not good going into election: Enda should come out fighting and face them down like Haughey would have.

HQ text: if contacted re current story please contact FG Press Office. Too late, guys: I gave a statement to the *Echo* in support of Enda. Time to focus on the election and on gaining momentum, not losing out to infighting over a radio interview that probably amounted to nothing.

Friday night is the eve of the Feast of the Epiphany, so we decide not to go out canvassing, as many would be gone to Mass.

Second text arrives from HQ: We understand that 'Prime Time' are looking to do a follow-up on the recent controversy and are contacting people. Enda has dealt with the matter and considers it closed.

Enough said.

Friday 5 January

Off to Dublin to collect leaflets from HQ. Met Ger, the FG printer, one of the greatest characters in the party. His wife is pregnant: 'There'll be no more leaflets for a while; you'll all have to wait. If my missus pops early, that's it; you can forget the newsletter.'

All I can think of is John and his reaction!

A boot full of new personal leaflets—prayers that Ger's wife will have a safe delivery, and that goes for my newsletter too. We are awaiting 41,000 newsletters, to be dropped by An Post in early February. The joys of being a candidate: leave Cork at 7:30 a.m., drive to Dublin, arrive at FG printing works, strike back for Cork. Oh, the joys, or perhaps, as many would think and say, a waste of precious time.

Monday 8 January

Random selection of quotes from the doorstep: 'I left Fine Gael in 1986 because of the prodivorce stance. I felt it was opening the flood gates. I hope you do well anyway. The people are fed up with politicians and all those expense accounts.'

'I'm glad you called. I think Enda Kenny is shooting himself in the foot.'

'I'm a floating voter. My father was on one side in the Civil War and my uncle was on the other side. Neither of them got recognition.'

'I give Peter Barry full credit for listening to me way back and I was one of the first to tell him that the Birmingham Six were innocent. And he took it up.'

'Do something about the street lights, will you? Are they fixing them? They've been out for a week.' (Not that there's any danger, with your three dogs.)

'You're a busy man in the GAA. You had one of the best seasons ever. I'll keep you in mind and have a word with my wife too.'

'Are you any relation of Frank Buttimer?'

'I'm looking for a house, a house in Togher; if you could do something for me you'll get my vote straight away.'

'I'm from Lithuania; nice to meet you.'

'I'm in second year in Coláiste Chríost Rí, I play under-fourteen with Nemo. My cousins the Galvins are out in Bishopstown. I'll read your leaflet.'

Wednesday 10 January

Cross Douglas Road. Canvassing again; man says he knows me. 'I met you at the Muskerry 1970 football team's 25th anniversary celebrations. My father is from Kilmichael, and the Muskerry team that won the county were the greatest thing in our house. There were newspaper cuttings and he always mentioned Noel Dunne, and my brother William's first words were Billy Morgan. I used to do commentary in the bedroom (and worked for local radio since).'

Another door: 'Because I'm a first-time voter and you're a first-time candidate I'll vote for you.' Better news.

Friday 12 January

Douglas Road, Baltimore, Rosebank, Whitethorn. The swimming pool is still an issue here. 'I won't vote for you because of Douglas Pool. I'd say the application wasn't in soon enough to get the money.'

So are dogs. 'Sorry, he'll run out if I don't hold him back. What are you going to do with the health service? Are you going to privatise it? I work in the health service. I'm not a consultant. I work in the laboratory, but we're being blamed for patients on trolleys.'

'Who is going with you? Simon Coveney and Deirdre Clune? I have my doubts about her.'

I feel the criticism unfair as Deirdre Clune is an assiduous worker and was an excellent lord mayor.

'Charlie is being murdered on "Coronation Street". If he's murdered now before I go back in I'll murder you.'

Saturday 13 January

Ballincurrig Park. The Douglas Swimming Pool is a big issue around here; there's a long-running campaign to keep it open—a very long-running campaign.

'I have a child who is eight. I was pregnant with her when we were protesting first. And I am still waiting. She will be married by the time it is sorted out.'

'My son swam in the Community Games and we have met people in Dundalk, where there is a beautiful pool. We started going there about five years ago and they were talking about applying for funding then.'

'They could do with opening a few more hours during the day.'

'What are you selling?—Only yourself; that's all right.'

'This is a German shepherd dog. If there's only a mouse at the door she loses it.'

'On your looks anyway you'd get my vote . . . Am I the first person that has said that?' You are.

Sunday 14 January

The first opinion poll of the new year is published in the *Sunday Tribune*. The poll shows that Fine Gael and Labour have gained support at the expense of Fianna Fáil. We face a huge challenge to overcome the Government, but it can be done. I always think that part of our trouble is our own misgivings at our policies and abilities to win elections. This election is going to be a battle in forty-three individual constituencies.

Fianna Fáil is at 39 per cent, Fine Gael at 22 per cent and Labour at 12 per cent. We and Labour are up two points, while Fianna Fáil has dropped three points.

When I hear of polls being published I always think of Charlie Haughey, who said there's only one poll that matters. Do people read polls and pay attention to their findings?

Satisfaction ratings of the party leaders continue to show Enda with a lower rating. This is always the way of FG leaders; is it that our voters expect more or is it that Enda is not performing?

Plenty to think about.

Monday 15 January

First full council meeting of new year. All of us are like school kids on the first day back. It's a busy afternoon meeting of Traveller Accommodation Committee and representations about other issues. The full council meeting is due at 5:30 and with it a new drama. The Kilcrea Lawn proposal is before us and also UCC students are in to meet a number of councillors. Sinn Féin's Jonathan O'Brien and I agree to go and meet the students to discuss the workings of local government.

Half way through the afternoon I feel unwell but soldier on. The sinus is a killer and hits me hard. Tonight is one of those episodes where it's a case of head down and off to bed.

Richard Bruton comes out very strong on Ireland as the most expensive country in Europe for consumers. Richard is launching our consumer week and promises to introduce new measures to protect the consumer; www.ripoff.ie had 400,000 hits last year; it's time for a consumer enforcer. Eddie Hobbs, move along; here we come!

Tuesday 16 January

Rhodaville estate, Rathmore Lawn. More local concerns: 'Between the Cross Douglas Road and the Douglas Shopping Centre every single road has ramps except for this road—we don't even have markings on the road.'

'The paths were not done and they're in a highly dangerous condition and we still haven't got any road markings, and we have all the traffic from Cork city going up this road. They're tearing up and they're even coming in from the top of the road and there's a sign "No entrance".'

'No, I'm up all day, the dressing-gown is cosy.'

'The GAA man? I'm Brian Dillons myself—I was a member of the first juvenile city board, Noel Callaghan and Father Nessan and all of them. The first match we played was outside in the hockey field in Douglas in the forties.'

'If you don't mind me asking, are you anything to Buttimer the butchers?'

'Dan Boyle said to me, If I get in, he says, I'll buy a pint for you up in the Briar Rose. Dan Boyle didn't. I'm waiting for him to come back.'

'I'm not a fluent Irish-speaker. I would love to be able to speak Irish, and I guarantee you Avril Doyle can't speak Irish.'

I agree with Enda's analysis of the Irish language in schools. It's not being taught in my view as a spoken language and I would very much support making it a living language. To me it's our national language and we as public representatives should enhance and develop it. I have never used Irish since Leaving Cert which I regret.

Wednesday 17 January

Adult education enrolment evening, so no canvass. It's an afternoon canvass with Michael Aherne as we amble along the South-Central Ward. Greenmount area of Cork city is an old and historic part of the city which was known as Gallows Green because hangings and other punishments were carried out here. One crescent of houses is Centenary Crescent, 1898. The name is in memory of the 1798 rebellion against English rule. The rebellion failed, and fifteen men were hanged at Gallows Green. When the Presentation Brothers came to Gallows Green they decided to change the name to Greenmount, because it wouldn't be nice to build a school at a place called after hanging people.

It's wet and showery, and as we start to canvass my good friend Councillor Dino Cregan calls me, enquiring as to how the canvass is going; he says it's 22 degrees where he is, in Spain. Well, Dino, it's 6 degrees here, showery and miserable, but there's canvassing to be carried out.

People are friendly: our first laugh of the day came from a semi-naked man who shouted at us from what appeared to be his bedroom window: 'I'm only out of the shower and I can't talk but if you're not FF leave the card.'

Another man won't be voting for FF but will be voting for Mícheál Martin; yet another wants us all to parade up and down O'Connell Street: 'You couldn't give ye away in a lucky bag.'

Thursday 18 January

Tramore Lawn. The first thing I see out here is the 'remains' of a previous politician.

'On this dog's bedpost is the leg of Batt O'Keeffe's best trousers that she got when he was coming in the gate. There was a fellow called around here knocking on doors for Batt. I had known him for years and we were away and I suppose Batt thought there was a constituency problem. As he came up the drive he never saw the dog inside the bush and she went for him. Batt can run!'

'You'd want to get your head examined now and take it a bit easier for yourself instead of getting into all that carry-on. Look at Mícheál Martin there, worn to a thread from it all and what thanks did he get? He's gone bald overnight nearly from it. Mind yourself. I'll be thinking about you and watching your head there when you get to the Dáil.'

Saturday 20 January

Fortress Thomond has been breached. The Munster home record has been broken by Leicester. Canvassing this afternoon is against the backdrop of the game, and at the back of our minds it's home and finish early so we can watch the Munster game.

It looked as if we wouldn't get out because of heavy showers, but they pass to allow Dan, Michael and I to set off on the South-East Ward canvass. Mindful that we are in the heart of Clune territory, we arrange to ask if people are committed for second-preference votes.

One voter is very insistent that she is voting against FF ('I'm very nervous that Bertie will go in with Sinn Féin. If he needs the number he'll do a deal') but the residents are warm and friendly. Meanwhile Hillary Clinton on her web site announces her plans to run for president in America.

Sunday 21 January

No canvassing for the moment on a Sunday. It's a time to catch up—this weekend we have in Bishopstown GAA Club the Johnnie Galvin Memorial Tournament final. Johnnie was a fun-filled young man, and my mum always told of meeting Johnnie coming home one night with one too many on board. As she said, it was the bike was bringing Johnnie home. He was a young man taken in his prime.

'This Week' interview with Enda: I love it when he says, 'The election will be the mother and father of all battles.' He is some campaigner. In the interview Enda came across as strong, solid and measured. He said he was committed to the Fine Gael alliance with Labour and possibly the Green Party, but he ruled out seeking the support of Sinn Féin in government. I am a republican and don't share the same antipathy to Sinn Féin as many of my colleagues do but nor do I condone or excuse violence, murder and crime.

Again Enda said there would be no increase in personal, corporate or capital tax. I feel this is important, as was Enda's challenge to the Taoiseach to engage in a public debate on crime before the next general election. Good one, leader; look around and you can see the fear in many elderly and not so. More and more as we canvass, people talk to us though the letter box or from the upstairs window. Is that the Ireland of 2007, afraid to open your door?

John Drennan article in *Sunday Independent* brings out the ire of many with his suggestion that we will gain only fourteen seats. I was happy to read that in Cork South-Central 'a swing to FG will see that the party's blue blood Deirdre Clune regaining her seat . . .'

Sunday night is the Carrigaline branch meeting. Sunday evening for a meeting; what next? Off I go. It's badly attended but nonetheless we have a good discussion.

Wednesday 24 January

Now you see it, now you don't. The demolition of the Deanrock flats in Togher was the high point of the day. Built as part of the NBA housing scheme, the demolition of the flats in Togher has been a hot political issue that now is thankfully off the table. It was a momentous day and I was pleased that Tom O'Sullivan, a long-time community activist, was present to witness the flats coming down.

Politically the NDP dominates the news; the Government have a whole lot of money, a whole lot of spending money. The question is, will the people be fooled by the promise and allure of big money? I wonder...

On a personal level I have great sympathy for Tony Killeen, who again has made the headlines about making representations on behalf of a constituent. In this case, though, the issue relates to the early release of a prisoner convicted of murder. It poses the great question in Irish politics: do we make representations or not? If we don't then we are perceived as being lazy, and if we do we're hard-working. It's a no-win situation. I am a great believer in the 'if you are entitled to it you receive it, if not, no,' but as a local councillor you have to make representation on behalf of people, otherwise you won't be elected. For all of us politicians that is the bottom line.

Canvassing in North-West Ward again this evening. What a tragedy to see so many houses along College and Magazine Road ruined by absentee landlords and students who don't care! Rag week in UCC and the roads are buzzing with students. The evening has been illuminated by a scantily clad student walking home with a traffic cone under her arm.

Unable to resist, I wonder aloud is this the new boy-friend. 'Yes, it is. He does what he's told, he doesn't talk, he's adaptable, and he just rolls over at my request.' Game, set and match; little wonder Dad was not impressed.

One woman raises the plight of fishermen, appealing that we do something for the industry— on the day that divers located the wreck of the *Honeydew II*.

Just when your day is done it's not; off to the Bishopstown GAA under-age AGM, the lifeblood of a club. Jim Ryng as chairman runs a great operation, assisted by so many volunteers; I wonder how the GPA and Government would feel about giving tax breaks

The candidates: Mary O'Leary of CHASE with Fine Gael, Labour, PD, Green and Sinn Féin candidates from Cork East and South-Central. That's me on the front right.

Outside the club in Bishopstown.

Rabbitte and fish. Pat in the English Market.

Dan Boyle, with the other Green Party candidates in Cork, at a press conference.

Simon Coveney shakes hands with Timothy Flynn on the bridge that marks the constituency boundary between South-Central and South-West.

Mícheál Martin, Bertie Ahern and John Donaghy keep abreast of the news at Wilton Shopping Centre.

Some days you just feel apprehensive.

John Minihan of the PDs canvassing the youth vote.

Canvassing at traffic lights.

Labour's battle bus, with two of the party's successful Cork candidates, Kathleen Lynch from North-Central and her brother-in-law Ciarán Lynch from South-Central. Despite a mighty effort, the Labour Party nationally stood still.

With Graham Geraghty and Enda.

Enda Kenny was everywhere in the campaign and delivered a wonderful result for Fine Gael.

to volunteers who invest so much of their time in training and in taking players to and from matches. I wonder.

Thursday 25 January

The preciousness of life was reinforced today when the Lord Mayor called to inform me of the death of Finbarr Allison who worked in corporate affairs in Cork City Hall. He was a lovely person, so capable and so helpful. Pat Gosh called him 'a true gentleman'.

Canvassing was scheduled for Borreenmana Road. Of course we brought the wrong register. To those of us involved in politics it's our guide book, and when we called to Clontymon Lawn it felt a bit strange. This was added to by the fact that a gentleman was adamant: 'Sorry, wrong constituency, we're Cork North-Central. I always get a card from Noel O'Flynn.'

All I can visualise is the headline in the *Echo*—'Buttimer canvasses in wrong area'—but quick as a flash I ask if he got one this year, to which his wife replies, 'Funny enough, no, we didn't.'

We ring Dino in Spain—he knows everything. 'Listen, boys, it's in South-Central.'

You sure, I ask sheepishly?

'Not only am I sure, I'm certain. Canvass away; slow it down and keep the doors open.'

The usual issues of health, MRSA, lack of bus service and affordable housing are raised. Cold night as the temperature lowers. The fun is good. We discuss the latest news on Tony Killeen. And Enda's hair . . .

Friday 26 January

'Here we go again, we're on our way to victory'—the words of a Wolfe Tones song used by a Cork minor team a few years ago on the journey to Croke Park. Ever since, that line has become a favourite of mine and I use it occasionally to motivate myself.

This evening it's just John and me canvassing in the South-East Ward. John is in his usual ebullient form, armed with notebooks, register, canvass card and torch. Off we embark on another evening of knocking and seeking support. Some American guru at the time of the Hugh Coveney by-election campaign in a presentation to us said that 90 per cent of what we do at elections is a waste of time, but finding that other 10 per cent is the key to unlocking electoral success. For me canvassing is the best way of meeting and conversing with people. I am struck each evening by the number of people who are alone, living in rented accommodation, at the increasing number of immigrants and at the fear of our elders to open the doors. I can understand that reluctance, especially on a dark winter's night, but the numbers who speak to us from an upstairs room is alarming.

It's a typical night canvassing, nothing too surreal; many quite content to vote FF and keep them in power. As we walk to the car I still remember the look on Hugh Coveney's face in June 1997 at the election count in Neptune Stadium when FF won the election and his comment: 'We have left them a pot of gold to spend and they will be in power for a long time.'

Tony Killeen in his fourteen years has sent out 200,000 letters. It's the way of Irish politics, represent or be voted out. I enjoyed Michael Ring on 'Morning Ireland': 'When people are in difficulty, the first two they turn to is the priest and politician; people expect us to be whiter than white but at the same time break every law in the land for them.' It's a conundrum for all of us.

Saturday 27 January

Canvassing today from 12 noon to 4 p.m. A small group, Catriona, Noel and I, head out on the morning canvass. Slow start to the day as many people are out and in the beginning those who answer are either just up, in the process of getting up or just not interested. All of this comes to an abrupt end when a lady lets fly at the FG approach to the Irish language. 'I'm very unhappy at the way you're treating the Irish language. It's terrible, we should be proud of it and support it more.'

Yes, I agree, and point out that is what Enda wants: a debate on the teaching of Irish in our schools, and is positive.

'Ye're not positive, ye're always negative, constantly being critical and never telling us what ye will do.'

Another irate homeowner forcibly tells us where to go: 'I'm sick of ye, I have no respect for any of you, I won't vote, I refuse to vote, ye're the greatest shower of wasters, there's too many of ye and ye only work half of the time. No, I won't vote, now go away and leave me alone. Ye're all the same.'

In ways the tribunal culture has damaged the body politic and has tarnished the name of politicians. For someone like me, who has never been offered a bribe, never been in a corporate tent, never received a gift from developers, it's easy to understand how people feel, yet, as Michael Ring said, they expect us to move mountains for them

It's the eve of the Sinn Féin ard-fheis, a momentous day tomorrow and one that will undoubtedly put pressure on Mr Paisley. We will see.

Sunday 28 January

Polls, polls, polls. The latest Red C *Sunday Business Post* has FG down and FF up. Here we go again, a see-saw of recent polls. Are the people telling lies? Or is it really the case that they are waiting in the long grass for the Government?

Disheartened by the poll, many members call to vent anger, frustration and surprise. Is it a post-NDP bounce or is it the case that people are happy and will vote FF? Remember, all we need is 3 out of 10 to vote for us; if this poll is a reflection—at 21 per cent—we will make little or no gains.

In reality the election will be about forty-three constituency battles. The poll is the highest for FF since the Red C series commenced and our lowest in a year. I received a text from a party member: 'We need to start picking up soon or the election will be over before it starts.' Undoubtedly morale is low and members are worried, but polls at this stage mean very little, other than the possibility that if a trend sets in it may influence undecided and floating voters. Personally it's a case of head down, keep knocking on doors and meet as many people as I can.

On the doors Enda is being pummelled: we hear claims that FG are too negative, constantly criticising the Government, lack of policies. 'You don't tell us what you will do.' It's the job of the opposition to oppose, to criticise, to point out the flaws, and to highlight an alternative. Do the people remember the way FF behaved when in opposition, John O'Donoghue repeatedly berating Nora Owen? As for negative campaigning, wasn't it FF who coined the slogan 'cutbacks hurt the old, the poor and the handicapped'? So what is different now?

Radio 1 is the preferred choice on the route to a friend's mother's funeral in Donegal. It's a marathon trek and the poll is being discussed. Marian Finucane's panel discussion on Enda raising immigration was interesting: John A. Murphy called it an 'impressive contribution to a topic people don't want to talk about publicly.'

Will courage do Enda any good? The need to have a real debate on the issue of immigration is necessary. The whole issue of schools and language support is one that requires immediate tackling in the interests of all students. Language is the currency used, therefore all students need to be able to converse in English. This is not happening, and it leads to frustration, despair and in time can create disciplinary problems in schools.

Monday 29 January

News broke this afternoon that Motorola were considering leaving Mahon. 'It is considering ending all engineering activities at its Cork facility.' The threat to 350 jobs is a huge blow to the workers, their families and to the region. It's a sign of the competition from low-cost economies compared with our growing high-cost one, and it's becoming a major issue. Workers are paying the price for the company's poor performance globally. The majority of workers here are at the high end and are third-level graduates.

Meetings in City Hall all afternoon, traffic issues on the Wilton Road occupied our minds for a long period. The residents of Wilton Gardens have a request for traffic lights turned down. To add to their woes there is a proposal that no right turn will be permitted out of the estate on the Wilton Road. Sometimes I wonder what engineers think of in planning routes. This route is the second-busiest in Cork city, with in excess of 25,000 cars using the road daily.

Canvassing tonight in the South-Central Ward. Joined by John, Sinéad, and Dad.

'Look at what happened today, there is no future for the country, places leaving Cork and what do we have instead, cheap labour and no jobs for our own.'

Our canvass would be straightforward apart from what happens at two doors.

'My late father persuaded me to use my vote, as if I didn't somebody else would. So now I go and spoil my vote, write a letter on the ballot paper. Ye're all the same. Not one of ye can run the health system—I had a great January: my VHI bill was €1,225.20 and my gas bill was €213. Very hard to keep going on that, isn't it?' By the end of our chat the lady made a promise to vote for me, a new candidate, though.

'More consultation, less arrogance' was the quote of the night from an elderly gentleman who was wound up about politics. No debate, no chat, just the line thrown at us like a mantra and away we went. It's partly true and a fault in Irish politics that we probably don't consult enough. Little wonder Hillary Clinton is engaging in a chat with the American voters.

Tuesday 30 January

Canvassing in Passage. Nice night. Mood is upbeat, despite the polls at weekend. The issues raised are local ones concerning no new school, public lighting and the need to look after stay-at-home mothers. 'If FG has a proposal to look after us you have my vote.'

Ethna Farr, a trojan campaigner and one of the people you should have in every party, and Councillor John Daly of the local branch accompany me as we travel around the estate. It's a good evening, plenty of reaction. People looking for change and the canvass is helped by the meeting of past pupils, old neighbours from Bishopstown. I'm glad John is missing, as he would not be impressed at our pace, but nonetheless it's enjoyable.

'The Government have let the country run out of control, we have a huge boom and people are on their uppers. Tax people on what they make.'

Mood is upbeat: Noel is in his usual gregarious mood: 'Speed up at doors; don't take too long. I know you have to meet people but don't spend all day at a door. It's 7:45 and we've only covered thirty houses, and ten were out, so at this rate we'll be here for the week.'

Labour and ourselves have published our new health policy. It's another joint policy document, again giving the impression of a seamless alternative Government in waiting. I'm confident that this will resonate with the public, as it is one issue that constantly gets mentioned on the doors. In fairness to all who work in the health service, something is not right, even though they work diligently.

Inundated with queries regarding the CAO web site. 'The Central Applications Office has urged students and others trying to log on to its web site to be patient and keep trying,' according to RTE news, but it's jammed constantly.

'Sir, what am I going to do? Is my life going to be ruined by this?'

Time to stay calm, don't panic.

News comes through that Northern Assembly elections will take place on 7 March. Good news, because a North that is peaceful is important.

Wednesday 31 January

Night in Ballinora. This area is close to my own, so name recognition is good, but, as Dan Ryan interjects, 'Boy, if you're not known here then where are you going?'

True enough. Still, as a new candidate there is this need inside: people must know you.

We meet a consultant who informs us of the day just finished: '8:15 arrive at CUH, 8:30 meeting, 9:15 emergency procedure—I had two out of five nurses out sick; no specialist cover; spent most of my morning trying to gain access to nursing cover. Afternoon spent doing ward rounds, had to source a bed for an acute patient and catch up on note work and patient files.'

Then the debt at Cork Airport is raised by a concerned voter who is afraid of the future.

Thursday 1 February

All politics is local, and tonight the Halldene-Benvoirlich-Curraheen Residents' Association host a Mass for deceased members of the estates. It's also Mum and Dad's anniversary. The first one without Mum; forty-one years ago today they were married. Mum is a huge void in our lives, and her spirit lives on and the acquaintances she met and her friends continue to regale us with stories of her life, her humour, her generosity and her wisdom.

Mass over, off on the canvass. Is it a bug? Is it madness? I feel guilty if I don't canvass.

A consultant and his wife berate us on the FG policy regarding co-location. 'I have invested in my future and I don't like your policy on co-location. Don't try to emulate the NHS in the UK. it's a failure, it's falling apart!' We agree to have a debate on it and to be positive on the work that consultants carry out in the health service.

Tonight is one of the few times I felt threatened out canvassing. An irate gentleman let fly at Dan and me. 'Oh, you're Fine Gael. You can get lost and take that Boy Scout from Mayo with you.'

'Pardon?' I said.

'You heard me. Enda Kenny brought Bertie's private life into the public arena and he is a disgrace.'

Dan and I protested, but this guy was not for turning. He became more hostile, to the point where I moved my notebook to my left hand and took a step back for fear of being struck. Dan was doing likewise. As the canvassing card was torn up I gently and politely asked for the number 2, which was too much: his face got redder and he just lost the plot. At which point we left the driveway in confident knowledge that we had secured no vote at all.

In his defence, he was honest that he would not vote for us.

Friday 2 February

No canvass. Mass in Cullen for Mum. Early evening strategy meeting. As a strategy group we met at the Fine Gael rooms at Bandon Road. This is a small two-roomed modern terrace house in one of the older parts of Cork. Not having an office of my own, these rooms became a central meeting point. In this office there is a framed print of Michael Collins, old election posters, and a certificate of honorary lifetime membership to one of my strategy team, Bill Murphy.

Gathered in the room and huddled around the Dimplex heater, it became evident that I needed to organise a second fund-raiser. This was essential for a number of reasons. First and foremost I needed to raise some money to offset some of the costs I had incurred to date and those I would have to face going into the election campaign. The money raised would not meet the full cost of the campaign or even a fraction of it, but it was still important to try to reduce the costs. The second reason for organising the event was to raise our media profile and to get some publicity. In running for election the old adage of 'no publicity is bad publicity' is certainly true. A well-organised event nearly always guaranteed a photograph in the local free press and, in all probability, the *Evening Echo*. The *Irish Examiner*, which is now aiming for a national readership, is more difficult to break into, but I always lived in hope. The third and perhaps most important reason was to increase my credibility as a serious candidate in the general election campaign, and this could happen only if we could get a 'heavyweight' speaker.

Having agreed the objectives for the event, we spent some time in reflective silence, trying to think of a speaker who would agree to come to a breakfast briefing, who would attract a paying audience, and who by their presence would lend credibility to my campaign. My clear recollection is that when John asked for a suggestion everyone said at once, 'How about Richard Bruton?' This was probably the first, last and only time that the strategy group agreed unanimously on any decision we had to make.

Richard Bruton is one of the most respected and highly thought-of members of the Fine Gael front bench, not only among the general membership of Fine Gael but, more importantly, among the general public and the media. As front-bench spokesperson on finance he has earned a reputation for clear thinking, straight talking and a concise, succinct presentation style. Given that the economy would be a central feature of any election campaign, having

Richard speak in Cork was going to be a coup. I've been fortunate to meet Richard on a number of occasions in the past, and he's also one of the most unassuming, pleasant guys you could hope to meet. Added to that the fact that he was one of only three Fine Gael TDs to retain their seats in Dublin, it was clear that he is a true political heavyweight. It was agreed that we would contact Richard and see if he would be available for the event.

Saturday 3 February

I rang Richard and was delighted that he agreed to do the event straight away, without hesitation. The only issue to be resolved was selecting a date that suited both him and me. Arranging this event with Richard, I quickly learned that he was a real operator and the consummate politician. Obviously a busy and successful politician; I came to realise why he retained his seat in 2002. I offered to book him return flights from Cork to Dublin, but Richard said to leave it with him.

Now that we had a speaker for the event, our next challenge is to advertise the event, organise media and sell tickets. Like my previous fund-raiser, I am very conscious of wanting my friends and colleagues from Fine Gael to be there but not wanting to place them in the invidious position of feeling that they had to support me. The other important consideration with this event is the need to broaden my base and to raise my profile in the wider community outside Fine Gael. Thankfully Tony Kennedy, Nicky Dunlea, Dino Cregan and his son Noel agree to join the fund-raising team. Now I feel happy, as I would not have the most extensive list of business contacts.

The Irish Nurses' Organisation and the Psychiatric Nurses' Organisation have voted 96 per cent in favour of industrial action, which will include a national work to rule, short work stoppages and lunchtime protests. Speaking to nurses, it is clear that they are unhappy and feel left behind. I can't help wondering are they pursuing the correct course. The nurses I have spoken to, many of them friends, are gung-ho looking for parity.

Canvass in Ballyphehane 12 noon to 5 with no break. Really feel the cold.

'To be honest, I won't bother to vote. No matter who I vote for ye all behave the same way; it's the same old story. It doesn't matter who is in power. If I vote FG ye can't go on your own so you need someone else, and I don't like Labour or the Greens. Have you read their finance policies? You would be better off staying on your own.'

It's the usual compendium of issues, health, local roads, traffic calming and the fact that we are out on doors in early February. At the YFG conference in Dublin, Enda called for 'a major initiative to tackle the growing problem of drug and alcohol abuse among schoolchildren.'

Enda is calling for schools to introduce random drug and alcohol testing, should be allowed to do so by the Department of Education and Science.

'Given the unprecedented pressure on our young people, the time is now right to empower young people, parents and schools in the fight against drugs and alcohol.'

Reaction from kids in school, I'm sure, will be mixed, but I think he is right.

Sunday 4 February

Week in politics. Focus group of undecided voters, second part of the programme discusses the issues dominating the election campaign.

Terry Prone, communications adviser, Ivan Yates, former Fine Gael minister, and Noel Whelan, political analyst, impress with their analysis of the focus group's findings.

Monday 5 February

At City Hall we have ward meetings. Cork city is divided into six wards. As a councillor for the South-West Ward I have, with my four other colleagues, to make a decision on what roads to be resurfaced. It's the annual road-resurfacing programme time. The engineers rate the roads and we either accept them or not. There is a debate about a number of roads, which are in poor condition, but in general we accept the engineers' ratings. Then it's a race to get the letters out ... I prefer to wait and attach the map and personalise the estate, while some of my other colleagues have a generic letter pre-printed. It's a matter of taste and what works best for you.

Off we go again, at most sixteen weeks to election if he calls it on 24 May or that week. Tonight is a cold, sharp night. You have to be impressed by the level of commitment of friends, family and party members who are prepared to engage in politics. Tonight is one of those nights; you might question their sanity—but I'm joking. I appreciate all they're doing.

Joined by Rita, Marguerite and Owen. Our canvass cards, torch to read the register and notebooks, we set off in search of number 1 votes or, as Dad now says, 'your highest preference.'

Tonight as we canvass, the benefit of the direct-mail leaflet drop is paying off; there is instant recognition and that makes a difference.

'I have come from France and what a joke this country now is, poor health services, inadequate child care and little or no public amenities. And you want me to vote?'

Locally the news is dominated by the total ban on visitors at Cork University Hospital because of the winter vomiting bug, while a ban also remains in place on two wards at St Finbarr's Hospital. I received a number of calls from people concerned at the condition of their relatives who are elderly.

A local robbery ended with the cash being rendered useless when a security mechanism sprayed pink dye on the notes. Now could you picture a robber on a push bike pedalling and pink dye spraying all over him?

My brother John, a keen art lover, is thrilled at the news that the artist Louis Le Brocquy is to be conferred with the freedom of Dublin.

Wednesday 7 February

No canvassing, as for once the Met Éireann warning of significant rainfall in the south is truly that: significant. Rain and lots of it is the order of the day. Not to worry, we have a strategy meeting at 9 p.m., a Fine Gael canvassing training evening.

Is the gamble about to pay off?

Mairéad Magennis is on course; the texts are flying all day. Buoyed by the poll results, speculation now looms on Mairéad being the new leader . . . Hello— hold on a bit, we have an election to win, and I am for Enda.

A new opinion poll reveals in Louth that Mairéad McGuinness is on 14 per cent, Fergus O'Dowd on 13 per cent, ahead of Jim Darcy on 5 per cent. We are on course to win two seats. Dermot Ahern is predicted to take 26 per cent of the vote, an increase of 5 per cent on 2002, when he again topped the poll. Séamus Kirk at 9 per cent is the likely casualty.

Sinn Féin's Arthur Morgan is on 16 per cent, and the others are Labour's Gerald Nash on 7 per cent, with Mark Dearey (Greens) on 6 per cent, Peter Short (Workers' Party) on 2 per cent and Fianna Fáil's third candidate, Frank Maher, at 1 per cent. It could be good news all round for us in Louth as, if Fergus O'Dowd is elected along with Mairéad, his brother Michael, the Mayor of Drogheda, would take her seat in Europe, as he is the first replacement on the Fine Gael list for the Euro east constituency.

Now, how do you work that out? Still, slow down, there's a long way to go yet.

Thursday 8 February

Canvass Maryborough Woods.
Day opened with news that almost five hundred jobs at Pfizer's Cork plants are at risk.

Work for a councillor candidate, while it's a means to an end, is always difficult. As a teacher I enjoy being with students, they are very honest and evaluate life as it is. No half measure, no spin. If a student sees it different from you they will tell you.

One can't just opt out from class and take calls and seek information but we have to do our best. The announcement today from Pfizer of the loss of 65 jobs in their Ringaskiddy plant by the end of the year joins a possible 320 job losses at Loughbeg and 160 more going at Little Island; if those two plants cannot be sold on as a going concern then that's a bad blow, particularly coming fast on the heels of Motorola. It's a concern that such job losses are coming so soon in the new year.

Tonight is the first of the pre-election rallies in Rochestown Park Hotel. There is a great buzz, excellent crowd. All the candidates are sitting in the front row and are introduced to the crowd. It reminds me of the Irish Nationwide team presentation in Croke Park at half-time in all-Ireland finals.

Some of my campaign team are irked at the fact that the FG Press Office issued a press statement for Deirdre Clune and Simon Coveney but not for me. Let it go.

Friday 9 February

The Bishopstown GAA club dinner. No canvass today. The club dinner is one of celebration, celebrating fifty years and two county titles. It's an enjoyable night, spent with friends and club members.

Saturday 10 February

Maryborough Woods. A wet Saturday for canvassing. Interesting in so far as a lot of people were out; it's very hard to keep motivated when people are not at home.

In his keynote address to the Labour Party conference at the Helix in Dublin, Rabbitte said that people are working but that the Government is not.

He used his televised leader's address to drop a Labour tax bombshell, committing the party to cutting the standard rate of tax from 20 per cent to 18 per cent within two years of being returned to Government. He said the resources were available but that the current coalition partners were committed only to cutting the top tax rate, which he said would benefit the well-off.

We receive a text from Press Office prior to his speech telling us of his move. It is a bold move, clearly designed to defuse Government claims that Labour is a high-tax party. He also stressed his five commitments for change if Labour forms part of the next Government: more hospital beds and gardaí on the beat, pre-school education for all children, help for first-time home-buyers, and the abolition of the means test for carers.

The Labour leader also bemoaned the pressures of life in modern Ireland, saying that people were on what he described as a 'gilded treadmill' of work, traffic and responsibility. And he accused Mary Harney of treating health as a market commodity rather than a community service and said that Labour would stop her plan for developing private hospitals on public land if it was in Government.

Barack Obama has declared that he is a candidate for the White House. I wonder will he be the first African-American candidate to win the presidency.

Sunday 11 February

No canvass. Today is a day of historic proportions: in a historic break with tradition the first rugby game was played in Croke Park. I was so proud of the GAA, an association I have been involved with all my life—in the main as an administrator, as I was so bad at playing. I love sport and regret that I had not the ability to play the games well. The volunteer, the player, the administrator—the whole GAA is one great organisation. Where else could you find a tent to cover all views?

I deeply resent those who say that the people in favour of opening up Croke Park are liberal, that we have not the GAA's interest at heart and that we will lose ground to other codes. The reality is that some of those in favour of keeping Croke Park closed are hypocrites and their actions and votes are not in tandem. I have never gone to an Irish soccer international, only once whilst on school tour went to a soccer game.

I have no interest in soccer; I look out for Cork City results and hope they win, and in truth guess I have never watched a full soccer international on TV. Rugby is a game I like and to me many of those who play and attend are GAA people. But today is a great day and I'm proud of Seán Kelly and of the GAA people who voted for change.

Monday 12 February

No canvass. City council meeting. City Hall is a fun place to be. I enjoy the debate and the banter on the floor of the chamber.

I propose a vote of congratulations to the GAA on the opening of Croke Park; this will not gain universal approval from many of my former GAA county board colleagues. I'm sure I'll receive a few barbed comments from the Fíor-Ghaels.

At question time I have placed a question to the City Manager regarding the legal ownership of the lands at the rear of Glasheen River. I use question time to raise and flag issues on behalf of constituents. It is an opportunity to question the city manager. It can be frustrating eliciting information from officials.

Cork City Council meets on the second and fourth Monday of each month, with committee meetings in between. The work load of a county or city councillor is seven days a week.

Tuesday 13 February

Canvass in Mount Oval Village, Rochestown. The main concern of the residents in this estate is the need for a primary school in the area.

The one major issue today in school centred on Cadbury having to recall some of their Easter egg products because their packaging does not carry a warning that they may contain traces of nuts. It was a source of amusement to the kids that a large company like Cadbury's would have to recall mini creme eggs.

'Sir, it's like how you eat them. It's why would you eat them now?'

But as I move to assure them that my brother-in-law Jerry works in the Cadbury's factory in Rathmore and his job needs their support the kids reassure me of their support for Cadbury's and we promise that we will buy the eggs. If only we could stop eating chocolate!

Canvassing this week is in Mount Oval. It's huge. Vast numbers of houses and I can't get over the number of houses rented out. New terrain, new territory. Reaction is mixed: mostly they're for Clune, Martin, McGrath and Coveney. The school or lack of it is a big issue and there is a well-organised campaign by the parents. Little wonder they keep saying, 'The first person to come back with a school gets our votes.'

The lack of a bus service and traffic gridlock are huge issues also.

Wednesday 14 February

After canvass in Croaghtmore Gardens, issue a press statement attacking Michael McGrath. We spent a happy Valentine's Day out canvassing. 'Will you be my Valentine?' was replaced by 'Can I be your Valentine number 1 vote?' We were struck by the number of people home and—being romantic—the aroma of candles, fresh flowers and home cooking.

News dominated by the Tánaiste and Minister for Justice Michael McDowell saying the costs for the tribunal on planning matters could top €1 billion and warning that the situation could not go on for ever. I agree, Tánaiste, but what are you guys afraid of?

Phone call from Press Office whilst out canvassing in afternoon. Nick Miller wanting to know would I issue a statement on the Taoiseach's comments and his apparent contradiction with a drug survey by Councillor Michael McGrath. Today, my first press release by FG in Dublin.

Mount Oval on Valentine's Night was cold, wet and miserable, with lots of young couples home. I kept saying, to the annoyance of John: 'Roses are red, violets are blue, how I wish you could vote for me. Can I be your Valentine in June or May?'

My press release:

TAOISEACH SHOULD LISTEN TO HIS OWN CANDIDATES ABOUT DRUGS

Fine Gael Cork South-Central candidate Councillor Jerry Buttimer has accused Taoiseach Bertie Ahern of burying his head in the sand about drugs after he claimed in the Dáil that drug abuse is not widespread, yet one of his own general election candidates has conducted a survey showing that one in five young Cork people have used cocaine.

That's according to Fine Gael Cork South Central candidate Jerry Buttimer, who called for an audit of young people's needs in Cork in order to encourage them to steer clear of drugs.

Bertie Ahern stood up in the Dáil this week and told Enda Kenny that drug use is not widespread in Ireland. The Taoiseach stated: 'I do not believe we should say crime is rampant and there are serious drug problems in every village, community and locality because that is not the case.'

The Taoiseach should listen to the members of his party, one of whom has conducted a survey showing that one in five Cork people between the ages of 18 and 35 had used cocaine. The survey was conducted by Councillor Michael McGrath who stated that 'cocaine use is now prevalent among the younger generation.'

Clearly the Taoiseach is in denial about the scale of the drugs problem, when one of his own candidates is highlighting 'the new fixation with cocaine'. Yet there is no other explanation for the surge in gangland killings and last year's record 26 gun murders.

Some young people in Cork are falling into drug and alcohol habits because of the lack of suitable alternative activities. The youth café in Ballinlough was closed recently and there is a serious shortage of activities in the city for those not interested in sport or drama.

As someone who works with young people, I believe there needs to be an audit of young people's needs in Cork city to find out what they want to do with their spare time. We need more youth cafés and drop-in centres. This audit should be conducted by all relevant bodies including the local authority, VECs, Department of Education and the HSE. At the same time we need to take a serious look at the way society is going in terms of alcohol and drug abuse. But we also need to ask whether the Taoiseach of this country should be allowed to ignore the scourge of drugs, when even members of his own party now acknowledge the scale of the problem.

Thursday 15 February

Mount Oval.
The row continues about the Planning Tribunal. The chairman of the tribunal, Alan Mahon, has said that the final cost of the inquiry will be €300 million and not the €1 billion suggested by the Tánaiste and Minister for Justice, Michael McDowell.

Interestingly, Mr Justice Mahon revealed that he wrote to the Clerk of the Dáil and in his letter he said the €300 million figure could be reduced if those found not to have co-operated with the inquiry had to pay their own legal bills.

Do we really know how much it will cost though? For many the tribunals have lost their relevance. Judge Mahon also insists that the tribunal should complete its remaining public hearings by early next year; he says he had advised the Minister for the Environment, Dick Roche, of this time scale in a letter two weeks ago. So why now do we have the Government stepping in with such glee and concerns over costs?

Friday 16 February

Mount Oval. One response: 'I hate telling lies—I've just been to Mass. To be honest with you I did vote Fianna Fáil in the last election. I don't think I will this time.'

Saturday 17 February

Greenwood, Robins Court, Togher. The PD conference is on in Wexford. The mood at the doors today is less than complimentary to them. Amazing how the pendulum has swung away from McDowell!

Met Councillor Gerry Kelly at a charity event. He was singing his new song on McDowell; it brought the house down. To the air of 'Moriarty' . . .

> My name is Michael McDowell, doing crosswords in the Dáil,
> And now I am the Tánaiste, supporting Fianna Fáil.
> I'm providing guards all over town—voluntary, you might say;
> The good news is they'll do the job and I don't have to pay.
>
> Then I'll take over health with a similar plan and I'll get more volunteers;
> Sure your neighbour there can look up your nose or even probe your ears.
> Imagine a country where you didn't have to wait for a hip or a knee or an eye:
> Just volunteer for the HSE and do it DIY.
>
> But now I'm afraid that my master plan might cause myself to fall,
> If the folk out there did volunteer for service in the Dáil.
> You see, they'd do my job, and without no pay I would have to disappear,
> And I'd curse the day that I did say, Bring on those volunteers.

Sunday 18 February

Michael McDowell has proposed cutting the standard and higher tax rates to 18 per cent and 38 per cent, respectively, during the lifetime of the next Government. Today was the last day that trucks with five or more axles could use Dublin city centre during daytime hours without a permit. I wonder what the M50 will be like tomorrow.

The 'This Week' programme had the Tánaiste and Progressive Democrat leader, Michael McDowell, on; he said he was prepared to do a coalition deal with any ideologically compatible party. Speaking on RTE Radio 'This Week', he said such a party could include Fine Gael, but only if they so wanted it. Mr McDowell said he was into conviction politics and not auction politics. Hello!

Canvassing in Togher area.

Monday 19 February

Robins Court, Togher. One constituent has problems with our party leader: 'Enda is not coming across as having the integrity and ability to lead the country. He just seems to be following. There is something about his personality.'

Criticism of Enda or any one of us is part of life as a politician, but what irritates me is that we rush to form judgments. In the case of Enda Kenny he has united FG, reformed the party structure, and reenergised the membership in three years. Today we have a fighting chance of government whereas in 2002 we were decimated.

Whatever else as a leader he is not a follower and has shown leadership.

Tuesday 20 February

Mount Oval, Rochestown. It's Pancake Tuesday and we are joined by YFG members, who bring youth and hilarity to the canvass.

The Minister for Transport, Martin Cullen, has said that it would be reasonable for Cork Airport to accept responsibility for €100 million of its debt burden but has ruled out higher airport charges to fund the debt. When plans to break up Aer Rianta were announced, Cork Airport was promised it would commence business debt-free.

PD Senator John Minihan is behaving like an opposition politician. Minihan, standing in Cork South-Central, said questions had to be asked about how committed the Government was to regional development. Well, John, you are a member of the Government parties, so why have you not raised it and got the debt promise honoured?

I release a statement:

> The decision by the Government not to honour its public commitment and promise to deliver

Cork Airport debt-free is another example of Cork and the people of Cork being marginalised.

The people of Cork can no longer trust FF and PDs and their hollow empty words and promises are false rhetoric. Again we have another example of false promises by Fianna Fáil not being honoured.

If the Government was serious in relation to joint up thinking, decentralisation and its National Development plan and spatial strategy, then Cork and the greater Southwest region would have an airport debt free and not a watered-down version.

Hope it sinks in.

Wednesday 21 February

Afternoon canvass in Gillabbey Street. I liked canvassing in this area, as it is one of the oldest parts of Cork. The Irish name is particularly striking: Sráid Mhainistir Ghiolla Aodha. It was once believed that St Finbarr lived most of his life in this area, between Gillabbey Rock and the site that now holds St Fin Barre's Cathedral.

Canvassing in the afternoon is enjoyable. Usually it's a tight group of Bill, Michael and myself. It's become customary to head out after school and canvass. Issue of students by night causing anti-social behaviour. 'We have no rest from them. They make noise by day and night.'

No night canvass. Strategy meeting in Bandon Road. Present: me, John, John Coughlan, Ger Slattery, Noel Cregan, Michael Aherne, Rita Cronin.

Thursday 22 February

Mount Oval. It's a great estate to canvass but it's vast. The cold wind bites us as we make our way through the development.

Dan and John drive us on. Mount Oval Village is a beautifully laid out development just outside the city. The estate agent's brochure doesn't do it justice when it states: 'The layout includes a large central core green area with lots of small cul-de-sac avenues terminating in smaller greens.' The house styles include four-bedroomed detached, four-bed semi-detached and a choice of three styles of three-bed semi-detached, together with the range of two and three-bed village houses. It has attractive village-style architecture, well-manicured green areas but no school and traffic calming. Lack of bus service and public lighting were the local issues. Mood for change was palpable.

One encounter tonight with a lady who had the winter vomiting bug. I was amazed that she opened the door, but she did.

'Hello. If I knew you were a politician I wouldn't have opened the door. Don't come near me: I have the winter vomiting bug. Don't want you to get it.'

Apologetic, I enquire after her welfare. The last thing I need is the winter vomiting bug—although a few suspects would be only too happy to see me laid low!

Out canvassing one has to be conscious of small children being put to sleep, the Champions League, soaps, and apathy towards politics and politicians. Tonight was no exception. We retire to the pub for a drink and a review of the night.

Friday 23 February

Mount Oval.
Can't change some people's minds: 'Am I looking for change, is that what you said? Well, they've been in power for the last ten years now and I know there have been scandals but they haven't done a bad job, like. They could possibly have done better all right. As I said, I will definitely go to Michael McGrath, he's the local man.'

Saturday 24 February

Monkswood, Kensingston Upper, Rochestown. Canvassing from 11:30 because of the big rugby game on later. The Six Nations game between Ireland and England is on the majority of people's minds, and not politics. It's a lovely spring day. Michael, Rita and I canvass. The pace is leisurely and the people polite, hospitable, almost surprised to see us.

Conscious of the game, we finish early to watch the game, which Ireland won easily, 43 to 13. It was some occasion: 82,000 people in Croke Park to watch an Irish rugby team play England. How times have changed!

Sunday 25–Tuesday 27 February

None.

Wednesday 28 February

Afternoon canvass in Reendowney Place, Ballyphehane.

Thursday 1 March

Afternoon canvass in Sharman Crawford Street, Cross's Green. Night in Pic-du-Jer Park, Ballinlough. Christine Cregan, daughter of Councillor Dino Cregan, is among our canvassers tonight. Christine is a bright light on a cold night. She has warmth and personality and knows everybody, or they all know her. 'Jerry, I should be the candidate, boy,' she kept telling me. To which I replied, 'Not a bother. Run in the locals first.' There was no reply.

Good response on the doors, people telling us they were sick of Fianna Fáil, angry with McDowell and concerned abut the health service. There is a mood for change but it's not crystallised to anybody or any party yet.

The question of Cork Airport raises its head again. Despite the claims of some Fianna Fáil politicians, this is not just a political issue. Tonight as we were out canvassing the CAA issued a statement stating that 'it would be hiring consultants to enable it to negotiate what it described as satisfactory terms and conditions with the Dublin Airport Authority and Department of Transport.' The bottom line is that there is a promise that Cork Airport would be debt-free when it gained its independence from Dublin.

Friday 2 March

Belmont and Beechwood Park, Ballinlough. The rain is pouring down as Noel and I trundle our way along the pavements. It's an old part of the city; the people are friendly and concerned about the roads, traffic and parking. Noel and I dart between the puddles and the rain as we canvass. Some of the comments include:

'Boys, ye'll get yer death. Have ye no sense? It's only March! Why are ye here?'

'Lads, I'm not staying at the door to get wet. Have ye not got an umbrella or a cap?'

Leaving that particular house, we smile and laugh, as we did have an umbrella. It was a Simon Coveney MEP one, but in our wisdom, or perhaps lack of it, we left it in the car.

The youth café in Ballinlough has been closed temporarily. It has become a huge local issue, polarising neighbours. The young people who met politicians petitioning to keep it open impressed me. I also understand where the community association is coming from. I would be very supportive of the need to establish youth cafés in communities. We need to offer young people facilities and an alternative to various sources of devilment.

Enda comes out strong in favour of Cork Airport when he says, 'The Government had made it perfectly clear that both Shannon and Cork would be debt-free as they face the future as independent airports. The proposal was another example of this Government not being able to honour its commitment in this case, and not being able to stand by its word.'

It's the weekend of the Sinn Féin ard-fheis. Not surprisingly, Martin McGuinness has said that 'the party stands ready for government.' That will be one of the biggest questions in the months ahead: will Sinn Féin be in a position to be a part of a coalition?

Saturday 3 March

Belmont Park, Somerton Park, Laurel Grove, Ballinlough. It's a sunny but cold Saturday afternoon as we continue our quest. It's days like today that you feel progress is being made. The name recognition is good, the interaction is positive and the mood is upbeat.

Because of it being the weekend of the Sinn Féin ard-fheis, many people spoke of their fear of having them in government. I have to say that I get on very well with Councillor Jonathan O'Brien. We work well together and in my opinion he is a good public representative. There will come a time when Sinn Féin will be in government; it's only a matter of time, and who with.

Sunday 4 March
None.

Monday 5 March

Canvass cancelled tonight because of the very wet weather.

Media in Cork are important. The impact of the *Cork Independent*, *Douglas Post* and *Douglas Weekly* cannot be underestimated. I enjoy Neil Prenderville's radio programme. He is the voice of Cork city. Most days he is topical, controversial and lively. After his show ends at noon, local radio is effectively finished, because all we have is wall-to-wall music. Oh to have RTE Radio Cork back on air!

The *Irish Examiner* and the *Evening Echo* are the two big media vehicles of Cork. The *Examiner* carries a good local section. The editorial policy has returned to covering Cork, thanks to Eoin English and Seán Riordan, who are approachable and interested in Cork stories. I may not always agree with them but they listen and are balanced. The *Evening Echo* is the city bible. Often people will tell you: 'I saw you on the *Echo*,' or 'I read what you had to say on the *Echo*.' It was on the *Echo*, so it must be true. If only Mary, Alison or Edel would be infallible.

PE facilities are in the news today. An EU report ranked Ireland close to the bottom in the provision of physical education in primary schools. Six out of ten are judged to have inadequate facilities and equipment. Fair play to Jimmy Deenihan, who carried out a survey on the state of facilities and timing for PE in schools. In today's climate of healthy life-style there can be no excuse for not timetabling sufficient time for PE. Seán Cottrell on radio today gave a good idea to teach PE through Irish. Good idea, and ties up nicely with Enda's Irish-language approach.

Tuesday 6 March

Canvass in Browningstown Park, Dryden Terrace, Pinewood. Tonight a lady asked me, 'Whose seat do you want to take?'

I answered: 'My own.'

'Oh, I know that,' she says, 'but Fine Gael will definitely win one and, if on a good day you're lucky, two. So who will you take out?'

Good question. The answer is, I don't care whose seat I win once I get elected.

Luckily in Cork South-Central the three candiates —Simon, Deirdre and I—have a good relationship. There is healthy competition but I sense no bitterness or hostility between us, whatever about the supporters. We work well together and each brings different strengths to the ticket. Obviously, being a first-time candidate, I feel under more pressure. I get annoyed at people who tend to look at me as the third candidate. I never look at it as me but as the team behind me. Each voluntarily canvassing, giving up free time.

This week canvassing in the South-East Ward is a different proposition. It's definitely Clune, Martin, Boyle and Coveney territory. Nonetheless the mood is good, the rain and cold won't deflect us as the reception for Team Buttimer is positive and enriching.

Wednesday 7 March

Afternoon canvass in Greenmount. It is wet and wild again tonight and we are back in Browningstown Park. We also canvass in Hettyfield and South Lodge. John and his team are canvassing in Riverview Estate, Glasheen, tonight.

The NI election dominates the news. It's going to be the big two, SF and DUP, who win out. Polls have closed in the Stormont Assembly elections in Northern Ireland, the third Assembly election since the Good Friday Agreement was negotiated and signed almost nine years ago.

CUH Maternity is in the news. The nurses have real fears over the move and I have met INO representatives. The one thing I have come to know is that Michael Dinneen of the INO is a guy whose judgement I would trust.

Cork obstetricians have called an emergency meeting tomorrow evening to discuss their concerns about patients' safety and staffing levels at the new Cork University Maternity Hospital, which is due to open in two weeks' time. Prof. John Higgins, who is chairman of the Division of Obstetrics, Gynaecology and Neonatology at the hospital, says their immediate concern is whether they can guarantee safety for all expectant mothers and patients with the closure of the city's three maternity hospitals and the opening of the hospital on 24 March. He says consultants at the new hospital do not yet know what staff they will have to work with when the new hospital opens.

He said it is not like opening a hotel. They need to be sure they can guarantee safety and be sure they have the actual staff levels to open the hospital—not just the staff needed in the long term to run the new service.

He also said that a contingency plan is needed to ensure the safe working transition of staff coming from three hospitals into one.

Thursday 8 March

Canvass in Nursery Drive and Lake Lawn. However, our canvass is halted by a bad bout of sinus, but not before I get an earful about class sizes and the fact that none of the parties is stepping up to the mark on looking after special-needs children.

News filters through that Motorola in Blackrock, on the south side of Cork and very much part of Cork South-Central, will be closed by the end of May. It's also announced that 330 of the 350 workers will lose their jobs.

Friday 9 March

This morning is my fund-raising breakfast in the Clarion Hotel, with Richard Bruton as the guest speaker; am canvassing in Ballinlough later.

Having organised fund-raising events for my GAA club on several occasions, I'm aware of the many pitfalls that can and do occur in organising events. One of these nearly did John's head in when he had many other issues on his mind.

For this particular event he was trying to estimate the number of people who would attend. The Clarion Hotel required this particular piece of information, and twice a day for a week and a half before the event John was fielding calls from the hotel. We just didn't know how many people were going to turn up on the morning, and because ten people were selling tickets it was difficult to collate the information.

As the date of the briefing approached I realised that the event was going to be successful in terms of sales, but as a group we still had no idea how many would turn up. In fairness to the hotel, they were very accommodating but needed to know how many staff to put on and how many breakfasts to cook. Three days before the event John, Noel and Ger had to set about ringing people to confirm attendance and to get names so as to organise a seating plan. Twelve hours to the event and I was still getting requests for tickets and people checking availability.

Last night John went to collect Richard Bruton from Cork Airport. True to his word, Richard had attended a constituency meeting that night and would be returning to Dublin early the following morning to attend another briefing in Dublin. John dropped Richard off at the Clarion Hotel to register. It was only the following morning that I heard that he had been upgraded from one of the usual bedrooms to the penthouse suite, where Diana Ross has stayed. Richard said that the room was lovely, and if only he had more time to explore it!

The breakfast morning was scheduled to commence at a quarter to eight, and by half past seven people were already starting to attend. I have to admit that the Clarion Hotel demonstrated their professionalism, as the layout and appearance of the two breakfast rooms was excellent. My strategy group had also come prepared and had table plans, literature and pre-election posters on display. The event was a clear statement that I was not in the election race just to make up the numbers but that I was there to win a seat.

Richard spoke extremely well that morning and had obviously spent some time researching the economic issues that were affecting Cork and the greater Cork area. He acknowledged the difficulty that Cork Airport was under in terms of the broken Fíanna Fáil promise on it being delivered debt-free, and raised the issue of the docklands, the need for greater resourcing of research and development and the need to forge and create greater links between the colleges and industry. He also spoke about the social, physical and health needs of our society and the fact that the Government should be judged not on how much they were spending but on the quality, or lack of perceived quality, of some of the public services.

It was a well-received presentation by those present. Richard and I were interviewed for two local radio stations, 96 FM and Red FM, and for the local press: the *Evening Echo*, *Cork Independent* and *Cork Weekly*. P. J. Coogan is a fair-minded journalist and gives local aspiring politicians a fair crack. I like P. J. and appreciate his and the 96 FM newsroom's fair-minded approach. Red FM, a new station in Cork, is also very balanced and I like the late-night 'Cork Talks Back'.

In many respects the fund-raiser marked the real beginning of the campaign, coming as it did early in the new year. We had ticked all the boxes, and people were beginning to sit up and take notice that Buttimer was in the race.

More than four hundred job losses were announced today in Cork and Dublin. In Dublin the CD and DVD manufacturing company Zomax announced it is closing its operation in Blanchardstown, with the loss of ninety-eight jobs. Canvass in Ardmahon estate tonight.

Saturday 10 March

Another weekend on the trail. The good news is that in the rugby match this afternoon Ireland won the Triple Crown.

Sunday 11 March

None.

Monday 12 March

Canvass in Ravenscourt.
Council meeting. It's Cheltenham week.

There's a bit of anxiety around because of rumours of an early election. Would it be a good thing to get it over with?

The Gardaí are angry at coverage of a mother's death; the Garda Commissioner, Noel Conroy, has rightly criticised how some media reported the death last Friday of the young woman who died after giving birth to twins. Garda Sergeant Tania Corcoran and one of her twins died in Our Lady of Lourdes Hospital in Drogheda on Thursday. Some media outlets had reported at the weekend that Tania Corcoran's husband, who is also a garda, was involved in the Abbeylara siege in which John Carty was killed. Conroy said the way the facts were reported in certain media outlets was disgusting, insensitive and hurtful. He's quite right.

Tuesday 13 March

Canvassing in the afternoon with Michael in Ballyphehane. We stop and look at the races in some of the residents' houses and share in the ecstasy of a win or in the agony of a loss.

Little did I think that I would be out canvassing in the streets of Cork South-Central watching Sublimity win the Champion Hurdle! My memory of the day is of an elderly gentleman bringing us in to watch the champion hurdle, showing me his docket, which had a significant bet on Brave Inca. As the race proceeded the smoke of the cigarette became intense, as did his roaring at Ruby Walsh aboard Brave Inca. It mattered little that the winner was an Irish one.

'The cold is perishing,' exclaimed Dan as we made our way around Calderwood. It's another evening on the trail. It's automatic now that we head off on the canvass. No question asked. John lines up the gang and away we go at the different points of the canvass. Dan keeps telling me, 'Some day, boy, you'll be a minister and you'll be in Cheltenham and not out here canvassing.' I smile, responding, 'Two chances: slim and none.'

Local issues are raised with us as we enjoy our canvass. A little boy refusing to go to bed for his mam asks us to read him a bedtime story. I promise him that if he goes to bed I'll come back at the end of the canvass and read him a story. He obliges and runs up the stairs. Winking, his mam says, 'Jesus, you're like all politicians, making a promise you won't keep.' I assure her I will come back.

Sure enough, at 9 p.m. I knock on the door, to be told, 'Shhhhhh, don't ring the bell—you'll wake the child.'

Wednesday 14 March

Canvass in Calderwood. John canvasses in Glendale estate. Strategy meeting in Bandon Road at 9 p.m. Tip O'Neill was correct in saying that 'all politics is local.' Tonight it was local issues to do with roads, traffic and public transport; very few people were interested in the national scene. I was struck by the feeling of detachment between residents and the local authority. Good local government means better provision of service, access to information, improved roads and paths.

The national issue raised was the publication by the Government of the Defence of Life and Property Bill. One gentleman was quite vocal. 'Do you think I'm going to stand back and let some gurrier steal my property or threaten my family? No way. Shoot first, ask questions later.'

Not agreeing with all his philosophy, I agree we do need to give protection back to the property-owner. Leaving him, I say, 'Don't shoot first.'

Thursday 15 March

Lyndon Crescent, Cherrygarth.
Class size in primary schools is more than an election issue: it's a reality for thousands of parents, children and teachers.

I attended the Cork meeting of the INTO series of public meetings on class size in primary schools. I was very impressed at the turn-out and at the high number of parents who have raised the issue on the doorsteps with me.

It is an extraordinary fact that Irish class sizes in primary schools are the second-highest in the EU. Commitments made five years ago in the programme for government to reduce class sizes for children under nine to less than twenty have not been honoured, they have been broken. The Government has reneged on its promises to reduce class sizes for the under-nines to less than twenty. Perhaps the old slogan should be changed to 'It's education, stupid.'

At present a quarter of all pupils in primary school are in classes of greater than thirty. Less than 15 per cent are in classes of fewer than twenty, the class size promised by the Government at the start of its term of office. In total, eighty-five out of every hundred primary school pupils are in classes above Government targets. People rightly ask how the current situation has been allowed to remain. The solution seems obvious: more teachers and more classroom space in which to teach. Everyone recognises that this cannot happen overnight, as it takes time to build classrooms. However, what the INTO and the secondary school unions are saying is the position is not acceptable, in that we have not seen a significant reduction in class sizes over the lifetime of this Government. Despite increasing resources and budget surpluses, class sizes remain high. What do we get? More SDP and whole-school evaluation. I could fill a room with paper on SDP and planning. For what?

Teaching has become more challenging. The curriculum has been changed, but it requires more interaction between teacher and pupil. Parents have more of a role in schools. The only one who is being left behind is the teacher, the one who is at the heart of the situation. It's a joke, the lack of support for teachers: greater emphasis is being placed on results and the integrity of the school day. Not a word about parents and their roles or children and their responsibilities.

In the words of the INTO, 'What we have today is children rightly being encouraged to think more independently and to act on their own initiative, as opposed to simply obeying the instructions of a teacher. This new approach is reliant on a teacher being able to give individual time to each child on a daily basis. Teachers are saying that this simply can't happen and won't work if class sizes are too big.'

In Cork we have the worst class size figures in the country. More than 14,000 children are in classes of more than 30 pupils. More than 2,000 children are in classes of more than 35 pupils. Is it any wonder then that the INTO meeting in Cork was well attended and was determined to make a strong statement?

Pity that they are so pro-FF. I know that won't go down well, and I have great regard for Denis Bohane, who is a brilliant person. But John Carr comes across as being so FF it's unbelievable.

Friday 16 March

Hollygarth. Eve of Patrick's Day. I'm now on unpaid leave.

Prawns and wine is what we are offered on our evening canvass. It's a good evening's work, lots of people out but a significant proportion are at home. Is it worth it? I wonder, but Dan as always is positive

'Look, boy, if you don't do this you will regret it. You are giving this one go and if you don't do whatever it takes you will always be sorry.'

The offer of wine and prawns is tempting. So we finish our canvass and head to Amicus with a few other friends for food. This is one of the best restaurants in Cork; it's the kind of place one can relax and unwind. The spare ribs and burger are to die for and tonight they were a treat. I really enjoyed the food.

Contemplation on the future as the big 40 looms.

Saturday 17 March

St Patrick's Day and there is no canvass; the parade and the Lord Mayor's ball.

Sunday 18 March

No canvass. Sunday, and my fortieth birthday. I don't do birthdays, but at 8 a.m. the morning after the Lord Mayor's ball I am awoken to the sound of two young girls singing 'Happy birthday to you, Uncle Jerry. You are old now,' says Sinéad.

Éabha chimes in for good measure: 'My dad says you're forty, and that's old.' Thanks, girls.

Today is a hard day. Mum's death and the fact that we are celebrating a milestone makes it harder.

Five people have been killed in four separate road accidents in Co. Donegal. On a day of celebration you think of the people killed and I recall the mother I met the other evening whose daughter was also killed. Life is precious and we should always be conscious of that fact. So often we take life for granted.

Monday 19 March

Afternoon canvass in Henry Street and Grattan Street. Night canvass in Carrigaline and Herons Wood.

The cold was incredible as we walked around. Bill Murphy was so enthusiastic that I just kept on going. I will never forget the cold in the inner city this afternoon. Oh, how I wish I was in some sun spot! As Bill kept saying, it will be worth it.

Not surprising, many were out, but those at home were full of chat.

Tuesday 20 March

Herons Wood. Tonight I'm reminded of the chanting at Cork games of 'Deano, Deano, Deano.' In political terms there is only one name on the lips, tongues and minds of the people of Carrigaline and that is the name of Michael McGrath, the local Fianna Fáil candidate.

John turns to me at one point and says, 'Should we put money on him?' I give him an 'Era, ya' look.

In between battling with the cold and trying not to be disheartened, along with talking to people about the issues facing a growing town like Carrigaline, I'm trying to make sense of the canvass. There's no doubt in my mind, despite the litany of issues and unhappiness with the Government, that Michael McGrath will win a seat. I'm certain of that, and it's only March.

Wednesday 21 March

Afternoon canvass in Connolly Road. Night canvass in Herons Wood. Council meetings. Ran into a group of Mícheál Martin's canvassers. Cordial encounter where we had a chat and agreed to canvass separate parts of the Estate.

Thursday 22 March

I love canvassing in Ballyphehane. The people are honest, direct and to the point. They don't pull any punches. You'll be under no illusion about where you stand. Today was no different.

Ramps erected as a traffic-calming measure have not been well received by some residents. 'Those ramps are like the jumps in the Grand National. They're too high, dangerous, and unlike the horse the car is not made to jump them. They need to be changed.'

Friday 23 March

Afternoon canvass in Pearse Road, Ballyphehane. Night canvass in Bridgemount, Carrigaline.

'To be honest with you now, when I heard there now that you're from Bishopstown . . . my mind is made up to vote for Michael McGrath. I don't know an awful lot about politics but we get leaflets in from him, I believe you do the same thing in Bishopstown. We get a leaflet in every month with the local news and that's as much as we get from anybody.

'I will certainly give you 1 or 2. Honest to God. I'm not happy with the Government about the airport. I think we have good strength in Cork with Mícheál Martin, you know. I think he has shown some power since Jack Lynch's day. I know he has done nothing for the airport. He did well in the health service, you know. I wouldn't mind a change, though.'

Saturday 24 March

Canvass in Bridgemount, Carrigaline, Seaview Court and Villas.

Soccer game in Croke Park.

Canvass Carrigaline.

FF ard-fheis in Dublin. It's the old story with the Bert, promise, promise, and connect with the people. The Taoiseach promised that if returned to Government his party would deliver a €4 billion tax package over the next five years to reduce the burden on middle and lower-income earners.

Here we go again. It's the pension, as Bertie swears he will increase the state pension to €300 a week. He made a number of commitments on health and crime. He also spoke about an 'ambitious tax package' which he said would 'eliminate inequality in the tax code.' Hold on; are you not the guys in power for the last ten years?

The Taoiseach ended in a rallying call by telling delegates to work harder than they had ever worked before in a run-up to the general election.

Join the gang.

Sunday 25 March

None. Day after FF ard-fheis.
It's all polls; has politics become totally poll-oriented?

SBP poll shows a drop in support for both Fianna Fáil and Labour and an increase in support for Sinn Féin. *Sunday Business Post* poll indicates a narrowing in the gap between the current Government and the alternative coalition of Fine Gael and Labour.

Pivotally, in my mind, the poll was taken before this weekend's Fianna Fáil ard-fheis but FF will be disappointed that they are down two points to 36 per cent support. We are up one point to 23 per cent, but Labour are down two to 12 per cent. The Greens are unchanged at 8 per cent and the PDs lose one point, down to 3 per cent. Sinn Féin are up three points to 10 per cent, while independents and others are up one to 8 per cent. At least we are up in the polls, albeit marginally.

Attended funeral of a colleague's father.

Monday 26 March

Canvass in Woodvale Road, Blackrock.
Meeting with Frank Flannery, national director of elections, Tom Curran, general secretary, Ken Whyte, constituency director of elections, and Dave

McCarthy, regional organiser, to discuss the FG poll in Cork South-Central.

It's like doing an exam: we wait to go into the room upstairs in the hotel in Mallow. It's a 'meet Cork people' day as other constituencies meet to get their figures.

On the way down John and I go over figures and say we need to be on or about 8; in the meeting the pleasantries are exchanged and they give us the data; that's all I want. I'm not worried about anything else.

Boyle on 11 per cent; Buttimer 4.8 per cent; Clune 12; Coveney 15; Cremin 4; Dennehy 6; Harris if he runs 2; Lynch 7; Martin 23; McGrath 14; Minihan ?

We are on 4.8. My initial reaction is a joke and I begin to speak, then John kicks me under the table. I remember: let him talk!

I start taking down the data as John unfurls question after question. Frank is gracious and in his distinct accent answers them. I'm looking at the faces to gauge reaction. It's like playing poker, only this time we have no cards—or at least we don't think the pack is right!

I am stunned by the poll on a number of fronts: the reaction on the doors is saying another thing entirely about our campaign. I do not accept that we are as low as 5 and I don't accept that Simon is so far ahead of Clune. I don't think Boyle is going as well as the polls are saying. I'm not getting him on the doors like I was early in the time.

Our vote has not improved in the rural or harbour area. The only consolation is the South-West Ward is holding firm.

John moves into spin control on the way home. We agree to keep the figures tight. If it comes out that we are so low it could be fatal.

Nonetheless we have grown from the last FG poll in 2006, which had us on 2, and from Simon's poll.

I feel that McGrath is that strong and still feel that there aren't two left-wing seats. So it's between Boyle and Lynch. If Boyle and the Greens are on a surge then Lynch can't be on for a seat, but I admire his work rate and his tenacity. I say to John, don't rule him out.

McGrath is strong in the county area but what do we do to get ourselves back in the race? That is the question.

Northern Ireland

The Irish and British governments have agreed to accommodate the new target date of 8 May for the restoration of power-sharing arrangements in Northern Ireland.

A Raidió na Gaeltachta opinion poll is giving the Greens a seat in the five-seat Galway West constituency in the general election. Éamon Ó Cuív (27 per cent), Frank Fahey (13 per cent), both of Fianna Fáil, are certain to take seats. Labour's Michael D. Higgins (11 per cent) and the Green Party's Niall Ó Brolcháin (11 per cent), with similar levels of support, are in line to take third and fourth seats.

The TNS-MRBI poll has predicted an extremely close contest for the fifth seat in the region, with Michael Crowe (FF) challenging the incumbent TDs Pádraic McCormack (FG) and Noel Grealish (PD) for the final seat.

The issue of greatest importance to the electorate of Galway West is that of health care and hospitals (42 per cent). Crime and law and order (26 per cent) is regarded as the second most important issue in the constituency, followed by roads (25 per cent).

Oh, boy, it's going to be some race. I like Pádraic McCormack and feel the poll is not accurate, given his work on the ground. I also like Fidelma and hope she can raise her figures; knowing her, I feel she can.

It's not a day for polls.

Tuesday 27 March

A sunny afternoon and we are canvassing in Corporation Buildings and also visit SHARE in Sheares Street. Night canvass is again in Woodvale Road and Ashleigh Drive.

Big news in Donegal is that Dinny McGinley confirmed that he has changed his mind about retiring at the election. That means bad news for my good friend Terence Slowey. Terence said he had decided to step down from the Fine Gael ticket, to ensure that Fine Gael retains its seat. I call Terence but don't get him. It must have been a difficult decision for him. Terence always has the best interests of the Fine Gael party before his own personal political ambition. Maybe I should have allowed a two-person ticket in South-Central. Would two candidates have been a better strategy? I can see some of the diehards blaming me if we win only one seat.

Wednesday 28 March

This afternoon there are hailstones falling and cold March winds blowing as we canvass in Pearse Place. In the news is the Galway water—residents of Galway are affected by the polluted water, which is undrinkable. Canvass in Linden Avenue, Blackrock, Silverdale Avenue and Drive.

According to a poll in Kildare, Fine Gael will fail to win a seat in Kildare South, the constituency of former party leader Alan Dukes. So what does this say if we cannot make a gain here?

Does it mean we are failing to make the impact necessary to win back a seat here, just outside Dublin? No—I feel from talking to the others that we are making ground across the country, that there is great momentum behind Enda, great unity and vitality. Local polls have a bias. This is one where we need to win.

The poll shows the three sitting TDs—Fianna Fáil's Seán Power and Seán Ó Fearghail and Labour's Jack Wall—looking good.

Our two candidates, Councillor Richard Daly and Alan Gillis, chairman of the board of management of Tallaght Hospital, are behind. I know the score, lads. Keep at it.

Richard is on 10 per cent of the first-preference vote, according to the poll, while Alan has 7 per cent. Come on, Rainsford, work the oracle.

'As such, Fine Gael simply take almost the same share of the vote from 2002, split between the two candidates sitting at this election, and don't manage to make any significant gains for the party,' said Conal O'Boyle, editor of the *Kildare Nationalist*.

Thursday 29 March

Afternoon canvass in Father Dominic Road and Kilreendowney Avenue. Night canvass is in Broadale.

'I am the grandmother. I live in Douglas. I am in your area too. We need a change. I live in Shamrock Lawn. I know Father Christy well. Our loss is your gain. He works very hard. Are you getting apathy on the doors? If ye get in will ye be left to pick up the pieces after Fianna Fáil? That is the danger.

'Fianna Fáil have done a lot of damage in Cork. Cork Airport. Bourns Electronics. I work in the public sector. I was a school teacher with the Inspectorate Department, primary. Are you primary or secondary?

Best of luck to you now. We know Deirdre Clune very well—we will give you number 2.'

Happy enough, I say, 'Thanks.'

Friday 30 March

It is a cold afternoon canvassing in Quaker Road. Located here is the Society of Friends (also known as the Quakers) graveyard.

Tonight we canvass in Elm Park, and talk is of the ard-fheis, which will take place tomorrow. I leave the canvass for half an hour to attend the removal of Mrs Patsy Cuthbert, RIP, a loyal Bishopstown GAA supporter whose family are all actively involved in the club.

Saturday 31 March

An early start as I drive to Dublin for the ard-fheis. It's a great social occasion. I'm looking forward to the event. As I leave I collect Dan. We leave earlier than the rest, as I am speaking on live TV on a health motion.

Drive up is quick, no traffic as we arrive in City West.

In make-up for TV—Holy God, as Miley would say, make-up.

Joe McHugh comes in, full of gags and laughter. He lightens the mood for many of us first-time candidates. I'm sitting next to Tom Hayes and Gerard Murphy. The crack is good.

I have to say vainly I enjoyed being up at the edge of the podium.

Show time, and Lucinda is the warm-up act. Tom Curran is looking on in pure adulation, or is it nerves —I'm not sure. Delighted for Lucinda that she has got the opportunity to star. She performs admirably.

Enda offers the voters a 'Contract for a Better Ireland' and promises not to seek re-election as Taoiseach if he failed to deliver it.

Simon McDonnell, Dan Ryan and I, along with the indefatigable Councillor Gerry Breen, have a good laugh that night. The mood is upbeat, with a great buzz.

Sunday 1 April

None.

Monday 2 April

Afternoon canvass in Friars Road. Met Father M. O'Connor on parish visitation for Holy Week. We canvass in Broadale at night. Issue of class sizes raised. 'I am voting for anyone who can reduce my class. I have thirty-six children in my class ... We are paying lip service to special needs and then we have the main body of the class being totally neglected. There are children slipping through the net.' I agree completely.

Tuesday 3 April

Afternoon canvass in Father Dominic Road. Night canvass in Broadale.

Conversation with an irate gentleman: 'I will put it this way. I don't care who is in there once we get those fuckers of Fianna Fáil out. I will help to do it. And Michael McDowell should be taken out and strung up by the balls. I am retired and have to pay through the nose for everything. You will get my support 100 per cent.'

Another voice: 'Fine Gael. That's okay. That is good. I have offered the party my services because I am absolutely up to here with the whole thing. You know you can't get out of Cork, you can't get into Cork and you can't drive around it. What do you plan to do personally for Cork?

'The whole thing now about Procter and Gamble, we were looking at that on the news this evening and they had Mícheál Martin and I just said to my husband, he has done nothing for us. I read in the paper the Minister for Tourism, more money is coming down to Kerry, whereas we don't have anybody. Get that debt written off and get a ferry. Is the ferry coming? Next year? This summer, really? We will be paddling it.'

Another example: 'I would be republican. Ye wouldn't be, in Fine Gael. Ye are not republican. How do you define a working-class person? Look at us on social welfare and paying service charges. How do you justify that? Are you on social welfare? On invalidity pension? Both of us are. We have put in for a waiver.

'You can forget about it. We are with Green Star now. They won't give us any waiver but the corporation will be at a loss there as well. The only time I ever had for Fine Gael was for Hugh Coveney. He was a gentleman, he was a nice fellow. I know when we were having trouble with my daughter's stamps, he came and he came back to the door again with it. How can Green Star provide our services for €260 and the City Hall is €280 plus?

'What is going to happen with the health service? I have a young fellow there, he is seven years old, he is suffering from tonsillitis every few weeks. He is on an antibiotic and he is a year and a half on the waiting list. It will be August before he sees a specialist who decides to take him into hospital to take his tonsils out. How can you justify that? How would ye work around that? I am not going to vote Fianna Fáil at all. Sinn Féin would be a strong voice in Government.'

Wednesday 4 April

The weather is cold and cloudy this afternoon as we canvass in Capwell Road, Derrynane Road and St Anne's Park. The nurses and the INO are in the news. Many people are out.

This is the first Tuesday of the month—children's allowance day, Noel Waters informs us, which means people will be out shopping, collecting money. Noel's informed knowledge of the people, the locality and the voting pattern of the locals is a huge help. Noel has been involved in FG for what seems like an eternity. He and Michael are full of banter as we canvass and the chat, humour and anecdotes keep me entertained. Noel is positive and encourages me on. The chemistry between us all is good, which helps.

Night canvass in Lissadell and Maryborough Court.

I am asked by a lady, 'Jerry, why should I vote for you anyway? Not just you, Fine Gael, like? What about the health system? It is a joke. What about MRSA?' I explain about my raising it with the HSE and on the *Echo* last night, and of Fergal Browne in the Seanad.

'I didn't get a chance to read you on the *Echo* last night about it. The health system is all bureaucracy as far as I can see. They seem to be taking up all the money, not the nurses. I think nurses are brilliant. I am a floating voter. I am Fianna Fáil normally but this time I would never put that Government back again. I'm not saying you will get it either. I won't guarantee it but I listened to you. You are saying something anyway, Jerry. I appreciate it.'

Thursday 5 April

Warm this afternoon. It is Holy Thursday and I am canvassing in Derrynane Road and Tory Top Road with Noel and Bill. We meet Father Kerry Murphy O'Connor, who is on his Holy Communion rounds; we pass pleasantries as we all go about our missionary journeys.

The Greens dominate the news cycle and get more headlines in calling for all-party co-operation on climate change. They are seeking a reduction of the country's carbon emissions by 3 per cent annually over the next ten years. Yeah, but who pays, and how do we do it? It's fine to be saying that, but what worries me is that they say 'tackling climate change will be a priority for them in any negotiations for the formation of a new Government.' What does this mean? Twelve months ago no-one knew what carbon footprint was.

Night canvass in Broadale.

Friday 6 April

Good Friday. No canvass. The crew took a decision not to canvass today. Went to Easter ceremonies. Always liked them from my time in Maynooth. Father Ronan Drury always gave a thought-provoking and insightful meditation on the Stations of the Cross.

Saturday 7 April

Easter Saturday. We canvass in Landsborough and Foxwood in Rochestown. Beautiful afternoon. Usual compendium of local issues: bus, school, and national ones like health. Inundated with requests for supplementary register forms. Can't understand the poor condition of the register.

Women starting to raise the issue of need for next Government to look after the stay-at-home mothers, child care and tax credits. E-mail Richard to ask him to look into this as part of our manifesto.

Sunday 8 April

Easter Sunday. Full marks to Dr John Neill for his courageous sermon this morning. It's about time somebody has the courage to speak up on behalf of the elderly. He told his congregation: 'Elderly people are terrified that they may become victims of crime and they are also afraid that they might fall ill and suffer neglect.'

It is a theme I can associate with, as elderly people are afraid to answer the door at night. Canvassing certain areas of the constituency night after night, upstairs and downstairs windows are opened by elderly people, unsure and afraid to open a door. Respect for our senior citizens is a value we should not allow to decline.

I watched the news coverage of the ninety-first anniversary of the 1916 Rising. I remember Canon Ó Dálaigh in Farranferris teaching us to always 'honour the memory of the leaders of 1916.' My grandfather Jerh Kelleher and my father instilled in me a real sense of the struggle for freedom and the importance of the Easter Rising and of the subsequent Civil War.

The proclamation of 1916 was, according to my grandfather, the most important document ever written in Ireland. I look at the Americans and the importance and respect they give to the pledge of allegiance and in the singing of their national anthem. To me our proclamation is as important. I love the words of the proclamation and have a copy of it on my classroom wall, along with Michael Collins.

IRISHMEN AND IRISHWOMEN: *In the name of God and of the dead generations from which she receives her old tradition of nationhood, Ireland, through us, summons her children to her flag and strikes for her freedom.*

Having organised and trained her manhood through her secret revolutionary organisation, the Irish Republican Brotherhood, and through her open military organisations, the Irish Volunteers and the Irish Citizen Army, having patiently perfected her discipline, having resolutely waited for the right moment to reveal itself, she now seizes that moment, and, supported by her exiled children in America and by gallant allies in Europe, but relying in the first on her own strength, she strikes in full confidence of victory.

We declare the right of the people of Ireland to the ownership of Ireland, and to the unfettered control of Irish destinies, to be sovereign and indefeasible. The long usurpation of that right by a foreign people and government has not extinguished the right, nor can it ever be extinguished except by the destruction of the Irish people. In every generation the Irish people have asserted their right to national freedom and sovereignty; six times during the past three hundred years they have asserted it in arms. Standing on that fundamental right and again asserting it in arms in the face of the world, we hereby proclaim the Irish Republic as a Sovereign Independent State, and we pledge our lives and the lives of our comrades-in-arms to the cause of its freedom, of its welfare, and of its exaltation among the nations.

It annoys me that people dismiss Fine Gael as being non-republican, when many of us are not. What I always admired about Liam Cosgrave, Garret, Peter Barry and John Bruton is that they always saw the bigger picture when it came to the national question. Albert Reynolds, in my world, was the first Fianna Fáil leader to recognise the importance of all sides.

John tells me that this is our last day off, as from next week we canvass seven days. So enjoy, enjoy . . . I love canvassing.

Monday 9 April

Bank holiday Monday and we canvass in the afternoon in Needham Place, Red Abbey Square and Margaret Street and Evergreen Buildings.

Quiet, eerie sort of day as we canvass, much to John's dismay. In a way he is correct, as the majority of residences are rented or empty, with people away for the weekend. Nonetheless I feel it's better to be out canvassing than sitting at home thinking if only we were out. 'All politics is local' seems to be the maxim today as local matters of residents' parking, bin collection, rubbish being dumped and housing are raised.

We canvass tonight in Passage.

The INTO annual conference, which began in Cork this evening, was addressed by Professor Tom

Collins, who wants 'to isolate 7 per cent of the country's wealth so that it can be solely used on education.' Good idea, Prof, but get Government to commit, and at whose expense is that done?

Tuesday 10 April

Afternoon canvass in Patrick Trahy Road and Edward Walsh Road. Tonight we canvass in Monkstown.

'Time of year again. No major issues. I suppose change is always good. The whole thing is changing economically anyway. Whether there are any new strategies in place by anybody to do anything about it. The jobs issue is huge. My husband lost his job in ADM. He is working again at the moment. The reality is that we are less competitive. The other thing is that there is so much employment caught up in construction if that is starting now. There is so much talk about renewable energy, but is there anything being done about it? We are not committed to voting for anyone. I hate the windmills when I go to west Cork. Could they not put wind turbines out there in the ocean and they are not spoiling anything. Who are you running with?

'Deirdre Clune and Simon Coveney? He has a dual mandate again, has he? Europe and Ireland. I work in the banking sector. It is like every industry, the cost-cutting. Huge changes since I started twenty years ago. Voting? I have no clue.'

Wednesday 11 April

Afternoon canvass in Pouladuff. Out with Stephen Spillane and Marguerite White.

Mixed reaction: 'Come here, boy, I won't be voting you at all, not even number 15.' 'You're all the same. I'm staying at home on the day of voting.'

Intrigued by the ASTI congress, where a motion to establish a policy of maximum class size of twenty for all subjects was passed. This is what we should have been doing all the time.

Night canvass in Waterpark in Carrigaline. Joined by Councillor John Collins. Good crew out tonight and the response was positive. McGrath and Coveney strong here. Mood for change in evidence. Lots of uncommitted people. Oh, Bertie, call the election!

Thursday 12 April

Doyle Road canvass in the afternoon. Canvass in Marina Park at night.

Bishopstown playing championship.

Met a woman with strong views: 'Now, how do you stand on the pro-life issue? So what do you do then when the book tells you vote another way? The people in Europe vote for abortion. What do you call her—whatever ... well, she didn't vote the other way. And there was a time when I would have been Fine Gael all my life. And from the time Garret FitzGerald arrived in ... It might well be that we now have abortion on demand in this country. This is the problem, you see, it's the party whip. Ye are all the same. This is the problem. You would make a great TD all right because you have the gift of the gab. That's true, no man or woman has the right to take away the life of another. We will be lucky if he calls us in. Sure look at the Twelve Apostles ...'

I just stare and say I'm pro-life.

She finishes: 'There's none of ye that way.'

You can't win.

Friday 13 April

Afternoon canvass in St Patrick's Road. Night canvass in Carrigaline: Willow Close, Laurel Avenue, the Pines.

'Hello, I'm Jerry Buttimer.'

'Oh, hello, Mr Buttimer. I have heard so much about you. I am uncommitted but looking for change. Would you like to meet my husband?'

'Yes, but you too are important,' I answer.

'Oh, it's no trouble, he'd love to meet you as he is more political than me.'

I say please, as I'm beckoned to follow the lady. I duly set off in pursuit of another vote as I walk through the house.

Into the kitchen, where my man is naked. On seeing me he reaches for a tea towel to cover the essentials. All I can say is, 'How are they hanging? I'm looking for your vote.'

To which he replies: 'If you leave now I will give you the number 1.'

I smile and say not a bother.

Saturday 14 April

Canvass in Owenabue, Carrigaline, in the morning and Waterpark in the afternoon.

'You are a new man. I hope ye do better than the other crowd. They are going to be very dodgy. No, I'm not going to vote for them. I'm definitely not voting Fianna Fáil anyway. All them what-do-you-call-its are coming in—foreigners. They have everything and we have nothing. Even the hairdresser now, I went down to the hairdresser yesterday and everyone was from—what do you call it, Poland. And down where my husband is working, he is working down in Bandon, they are all Polish. That's unreal, like. I was in England there a few weeks ago, Liverpool. I love Liverpool, like, and we were staying in this hotel and there wasn't wan Polish person there. Not even wan. All English.'

Sunday 15 April

Sunday evening canvass in Passage, in Pembroke Wood in Passage.

Good response. Many young couples and a host of issues. People looking for change but they are voting for the local candidate, Michael McGrath. John and I wonder should we try to connect McGrath to FF more explicitly. After all, a vote for McGrath is a vote for FF.

Lovely evening and we are thrilled with the response in an area where my profile would not have been high.

Monday 16 April

Connolly Park, Pouladuff, canvass in the afternoon. Night canvass in Seven Oaks and Dunvale, Grange, Douglas.

One woman shouts out the window: 'I can't come down, I'm in the shower.'

'It's all right,' says Micheal. 'He doesn't want you, just your vote.'

'Oh, is that all? I'm fifty and in good condition, I'll have you know.'

'I know you are,' I chip in.

'I am. Do you want to see more?'

No, I say, nice to see you—sorry, meet you; I ask her not to forget me on the day.

Tuesday 17 April

Morning in Upper Friars Road. Afternoon in Glencoo Park and Lawn and Clanricarde estate. Night canvass in Parkgate.

West Cork nurses' stoppage. Great picture of Denis Donovan and Paddy Sheehan on *Echo*. Okay, Deputy Donovan, you can't be part of the Government party and at the same time support the nurses. Is it opportunism or good politics? I know Noel O'Flynn and John McGuinness in Kilkenny do it, but is it right, I wonder?

Cork North-West poll shows that we will win one seat with Michael Creed and that FF will hold two, Michael Moynihan and Batt O'Keeffe.

Dáil returns from Easter recess. I wonder will I be part of the next one. I was very happy with canvass tonight and today. Mood is good in camp. Upbeat and driving on.

Wednesday 18 April

Morning canvass in O'Connell Avenue. Afternoon in Glencoo Gardens and Lower Pouladuff. Night canvass in Bellevue.

Thursday 19 April

Morning in Lower Pouladuff Road. Afternoon in Capwell Road.

Met an elderly lady today who gave me an earful on the closure of local services for elderly, like post offices. She was right: post offices across Cork are being closed by stealth, depriving communities of an essential service and forcing older people to travel lengthy distances to collect their pension. All of this has been done without consultation or debate.

Three post offices will have closed in the south city area within twenty-four months. Dennehy's Cross post office has closed, Bishopstown post office shut recently and moved to Wilton Shopping Centre, and Carrigrohane post office means that a vast area of the south side of Cork is served by one post office. If you start at Carrigrohane Road, drive to Model Farm Road, take in Dennehy's Cross and Bishopstown, all you have now is one post office located at Wilton Shopping Centre to cater for thousands of people. This is crazy and is not good enough.

This trend is being replicated right across the country, with post offices being closed by stealth. This deprives communities of an essential service, and oldest people are being hardest hit. Not only do older people depend on their local post office to collect their pension, it also provides an important social outlet. Many older people combine a trip to the post office on pension day with other activities, such as active retirement groups and church services. Worst of all, the ongoing closure of post offices is forcing many older people to travel miles by bus in order to collect their pension, cross busy roads, and makes them feel insecure.

Post offices are at the heart of the community, particularly for older generations. I believe post offices could, and should, have a role to play in the future, including the provision of additional banking services. But let's have consultation with the residents and the postmaster.

Evening canvass in Rochestown.

Friday 20 April

Morning and afternoon in Killeenreendowney Avenue, Plunkett Road and Fairy Lawn. Night canvass in Rochestown.

This evening John and I were out and we called to the house of a very exact elderly gentleman. He was quite formal in his use of tone and language and I could see John almost standing to attention. To be honest, I could feel my posture changing to shoulders back, chest out and feet shoulder-width apart.

We spoke about the decline in maritime shipping and then he revealed he had a very particular problem but was confident that I could do nothing to help him. Eager to impress, I suggested that if he told me I might. The problem was that because his boat was of a particular size he could not get it upriver with all the bridges. As problems go I would have ranked it as one of the lower-priority ones, but his tone was so earnest and serious that I could see John shaking slightly and beginning to smile. I made some comment of empathy and said I would write to the city engineer on his behalf. Making a hasty retreat, I asked John what he made of the man and the issue going out the driveway.

John said nothing and I again asked what he thought. It was only when we had passed the window of the house that John turned to me and saluted, saying, 'Yes, sir. Blow up the bridges and make way for the officer's boat, sir.'

In that comment he had reflected exactly what I thought, and both of us fell about the place laughing.

Saturday 21 April

Morning canvass in Gregg Road. Afternoon in Rochestown. Night canvass in Grange.

Sunday 22 April

Canvass in Harbour Heights, Pembroke Heights, Passage and the Ovals, Rochestown.

SBP poll: we are up four to 27. FF on 35 are down a point. Labour down one to 11. Greens on 9; SF on 8, down two, and PDs on 3; others 7.

We travel to Dublin to see Uncle Andy, but on the train home news comes through that he's died. It's been a tough twelve months on Dad, losing Mum and now his brother, our Uncle Andy. Uncle Andy was warm, gregarious, outgoing, never in a bad mood and was always up for a laugh. He lived in Taghmon, Co. Wexford but loved to come home to Cork.

Monday 23 April

There is no family members' canvass tonight as all the family travel to Wexford for the removal and funeral of our late Uncle Andy. The night of the funeral we had a team of about 16–18 people out canvassing in Elm Vale. When I got back, Dan told me of events that happened that night. This is his account:

It was raining the same evening; the canvassers' group were divided up into two groups, about eight on each side of the road in the estate, two people to a door; as normal we knocked at each door, and when there was no response, I told them to date the canvassing card, write a note on it and drop in the letterbox.

This particular house was on the corner on the way in. There was no reply at this house, so we just dropped in the leaflet. We continued to canvass all the houses down along the road of the estate. When we were walking back up, this guy was out on the road, accusing us of not knocking on his door, and how dare we drop something in with a note when we didn't even knock on his door, so Dan really went for it: 'Your doorbell was rang twice and when there was no response, we dropped in the leaflet.'

Dan added later to me: 'He was having none of it and called out his son to tell us that we didn't ring the bell, so I let him have it and I was having none of his cheek, as I knew we were right and he was wrong, as this is not the way we canvass. He said that he wanted to contact you but I told him that you were at your uncle's funeral. The guy just wanted to have an argument.'

Tuesday 24 April

Canvass in Fernwood Crescent, Alderbrook and Palmbury.

Launch our latest leaflet:

NEED TO END LEGACY OF BROKEN PROMISES

Under the current government trust between the people and public representatives has been eroded as major promises have been broken. The Fianna Fáil slogan in 2002 was 'A lot done, more to do' when in fact it should have read 'Promises made—promises broken'.

Fianna Fáil-PD Report Card on Broken Promises

PROMISED	End Hospital Waiting Lists
REALITY	29,000 still waiting
PROMISED	Close Prison Revolving Door
REALITY	3,000 out on early release
PROMISED	200,000 extra medical cards
REALITY	Under 40,000 delivered
PROMISED	Primary class sizes below 20
REALITY	110,000 in classes over 30
PROMISED	2,000 extra Gardaí
REALITY	Under 1,200 delivered
PROMISED	3,000 new hospital beds
REALITY	Under 1,000 delivered

PROMISED	Value for money in Government projects
REALITY	PPARS, M50, E-voting
PROMISED	'World class' health service
REALITY	Health Service in shambles

Fine Gael is determined to end the era of broken promises and give the people the public services they deserve, underpinned by real and tangible commitments. The choice at this election is between more of the same broken promises on health, crime and waste of money or the Contract that will deliver health services that work, safer streets and accountability in public spending.

Wednesday 25 April

Canvass in Mathew Hill. Issue of autism is again raised.

The only current regional assessment centre in Marion House, Togher, has a waiting list approaching 18–24 months. The difficulty in the main has been caused by the Government's embargo on the recruitment of professionals allied to medicine—physios, occupational therapists, speech and language therapists and psychologists.

I've come across an average of two cases of families with autism a night while canvassing. There has been a significant rise in the prevalence of autism in the past ten years but this has not been matched by the development or roll-out of services. There is an urgent need to address the plight of hundreds of children waiting for assessment for the diagnosis of autism.

Parents are forced to spend upwards of a thousand euros for private assessments in Dublin, Belfast and Britain, while children on the public waiting list have to wait upwards of eighteen months to be seen.

There is currently only one diagnostic centre in the HSE Southern Region and this is not able to cope with the demand. It is essential that there are at least three assessment and intervention centres in Cork to meet the increased need for these essential services.

If elected to Government, I will call on Fine Gael to lift the current recruitment embargo of psychologists, speech and language therapists and occupational therapists, who are essential members for a team diagnosis of autism.

Early assessment and diagnosis is essential if children with autism are to have any chance of successful integration and participation in society. The reality is that many parents are forced to sue the state for appropriate educational provision.

We will be judged by how we treat the most vulnerable in our society. The current system is one which does not acknowledge the needs or rights of children or their parents. It is time to change the way in which services are delivered to make them more child and family-centred and friendly.

Thursday 26 April

Morning canvass in Curraheen village. Afternoon in Windmill Road and High Street. Air of anticipation as text messages are sent back and forth saying Bertie is about to call the election. One woman told us matter-of-factly, 'He has told the Ceann Comhairle to be free in the afternoon.' Dave McCarthy calls to say be ready; he could go today as the President is due to go away at weekend.

I'm conscious that we could be on the edge of the election being called and I'm pumped up.

Canvass in Trabeg Lawn at night. I later go to the Imperial Hotel to participate in the Vincent Browne programme which features all the candidates in Cork South-Central.

Friday 27 April

Morning canvass in Summerhill South. Afternoon in Mahon. Canvass in Glencurrig and Greenhills estate at night.

Echo Red C poll is the big news. Tension is high all morning. The poll could either make or break us in the eyes of neutrals or swing voters. It's important that we are in the race. I feel we are and despite being anxious feel, no matter what, we are in the race. John has other ideas and Dad sticks to his traditional line: forget the polls, they're not worth the paper they are written on.

I am encouraged by the poll which is indicative of previous polls which suggest an increase in general support for FG and for me. The poll shows a shift in momentum to Fine Gael and to me. Local polls tend to favour established names and under-estimate new candidates like me. I am pleased that my percentage share of the vote is growing and I am confident that Fine Gael and I can win two seats. The poll confirms that there is movement towards me and the party. I still think that there is a second FG seat and I will be working hard to win that seat. I am pleased that my campaign to date has made an impact on the people and I will be working harder than ever to increase my and Fine Gael's vote. There is a need for an alternative Government and that can't happen without Fine Gael.

From *Echo* (Commentary):

> It's all to play for with 7% drop in FF support but the party holds three seats.
> The *Evening Echo* Red C poll for Cork South Central shows a fall of 7% for Fianna Fáil from

49% to 42%. Fine Gael increase their vote (19% to 26%) but still only secure one seat while Fianna Fáil retains its three seats. Ciarán Lynch increases the Labour vote from 5% to 9% and challenges Michael McGrath (FF) for the last seat. Sinn Féin increase their vote from 4% to 7% while the PDs only manage to secure 2%.

Minister Mícheál Martin suffers a drop in his vote from 27% to 20% but still comfortably secures the first seat. Simon Coveney (FG) and Dan Boyle (Green) both increase their vote from 9% to 14%. John Dennehy (FF) and Michael McGrath (FF) both secure 11%; Ciarán Lynch (Lab) gets 9%; Henry Cremin (SF) 7%. Senator John Minihan (PD) secures a disappointing 2% while Independent Morgan Stack gets less than 1%.

The FG tactic of running three candidates would seem to have misfired. Simon Coveney does very well (up from 9% to 14%) but it leaves Deirdre Clune and Jerry Buttimer each on 6% which is not enough to see either challenge for a second seat. The challenge for the last seat comes from Ciarán Lynch of Labour losing out to Councillor Michael McGrath (FF).

The sequence of elimination will be critical to the result. At the end of the third count Buttimer and Clune are on an identical vote and Cremin (SF) is only 250 votes behind. As the contest heats up over the next number of weeks it is possible for any of these candidates to improve their position and change the destination of the last seat. It is always a challenge for Fianna Fáil to hold the third seat here, securing it on a recount the last time by six votes, but could do it again.

Saturday 28 April

Morning canvass in Ballygarvan. Afternoon canvass in Richmond estate, Temple Hill Lawn and Avondale Park.

Buoyed by the poll, there is an upbeat mood in the camp. It's all to play for. We are not out and we are certainly at the races. Now if only we can be taken seriously by the media commentators. Dad continues to say ignore the polls. Yeah, but if you're not in the game then there is nowhere to go.

I am happy that we're in the game. Now we can say, backed up, that we are a genuine contender.

Sunday 29 April

Text messages all morning; so much for sleep. 'Ahern expected at Áras in the next hour or so to dissolve the 29th Dáil. The election is starting today . . .' This is it: after my three years of active public representation we are off.

The election is called by Taoiseach Bertie Ahern for Thursday 24 May. We are canvassing at Masses in Curraheen parish.

I receive a phone call from Senator Sheila Terry who is in Cork today and offers to go canvassing with me this evening in Shamrock Lawn in Douglas.

Enda rallies the troops with a text message: 'You've waited five years for this. I am proud of every one of you. Go do your duty for the next three weeks and you will put FG into Government. Good Luck. Enda.'

I and a small team go canvassing in Shamrock Lawn and true to her word Senator Sheila Terry and her husband Michael arrive to join us on the campaign. I am very pleased that Sheila would take time to come out and assist.

At one of the first doors we knock on we meet a young lady from Galway, who subsequently joined us on the election train for every night of the campaign. Emma came to be a valuable member of the team.

Monday 30 April

We meet at 7:30 a.m. by Cork University Hospital on this sunny morning and hand out canvassing leaflets for an hour to the motorists stopped in traffic. Morning and afternoon canvass in Mahon. Night canvass in Carrigaline: Maurland,

Forest Park and Clevedon. Change, change, get them out—that's the early morning response.

While it appears random and unplanned, all politicians and political parties put a great deal of time and effort into the design of posters. Within Cork South-Central there was a delay in getting the posters because of a clerical mix-up over the issuing or cashing of cheques beyond the control of anyone locally. It was my understanding that posters had been ordered at the constituency level in January and that they were to arrive in Cork by April. However, our posters did not arrive until after the calling of the election by An Taoiseach. Today!

My strategy team are getting extremely anxious as the main vantage points across the city were being taken by posters of other political parties. As a new candidate, name recognition and facial recognition were key elements in our strategy and posters formed a key part of this plan. Now two days into the campaign and there were still no posters up in Cork. It's difficult to describe the feeling of helplessness that can be experienced when you know what needs to be done but are powerless to do anything about it. At least Deirdre and Simon were in a similar position as me. The constituency strategy group had the responsibility for ordering collectively the election posters and official canvass cards for the three of us.

As a team we all had a reasonable amount of experience of involvement in election campaigns.

Noel Cregan's father, Dino, ran in two general elections as well as numerous local elections. I had contested the local elections in 2004, been director of elections for Cork South-Central in 2002 as well a leading role in other elections at local and national level. John had been very involved with the Deirdre Clune election team in 2002 and Dino's local election campaign in 1999 and my local election in '04. John Coughlan had worked on local and general election campaigns in Cork North-Central. Then there were Michael Aherne and Bill Murphy, two stalwarts of the Fine Gael party in Cork, both of whom had either canvassed or been part of every electoral campaign in Cork going back fifty years. We knew how many posters we should be getting and where we wanted them to go.

Running elections is about getting support from as many people as possible as there are literally hundreds of jobs to be done. For a variety of reasons some people are reluctant to canvass. For some it's a fear of getting abuse at doors, of not knowing what to say, of being recognised, or of dogs.

I was extremely fortunate that I had a number of people who fell into this category but they were wiling to help in other ways, putting up posters or leaflet-dropping. My strategy team had identified a number of poster teams who would be willing to put up the posters once they arrived. In the run-up to the launch of the official campaign we received word that posters were due in Cork; on each occasion some hitch would occur and the posters didn't arrive.

Finally I got word from Ken that the larger posters had arrived and that the pole posters would be arriving later in the week. The posters were being stored in a central depot and all we had to do was go and collect them. For the uninitiated the posters from a distance look small, neat and tidy. Up close and personal they're larger than life. Our large posters were eight foot by four foot and four foot by four foot.

Derek Cregan, a long-time friend, offered to go and collect them in his van but unfortunately they were too large to fit in the back of it. This left our plan slightly unhinged, as we had hoped to use Derek's van to transport them to the various sites we had identified. Fortunately for us, Ken had recently acquired a trailer and kindly offered us the use of it for transporting the posters. The trailer was to become a permanent feature outside the family home in Bishopstown or as an attachment to either John's, William's or my father's car for the following three weeks.

In politics you do have to rely on the generosity of friends, neighbours and relations and it's at times like this you know who your friends and supporters are.

John and my father ferried the posters from the central depot to our home in Bishopstown. In total three trips were made transferring the posters back and forth. The posters were separated in the back garden at home into two groups, individual posters and team posters. We had worked out a schedule as to how and where we would distribute these over the three to four weeks of the campaign.

Even though we were champing at the bit to get them up we had to go canvassing first. For the majority of our team, canvassing was identified as the most important activity, as the time periods for canvassing were narrow and defined. It is generally considered that canvassing after nine is unacceptable unless it's a personal canvass, but posters can be put up at any time.

Canvassing finished at nine and it must have been ten or half past before the first poster team were ready to go off. William, my brother, had commitments at home and was late joining John and Noel, who had started off. For these large posters the lads had decided to start off in Carrigaline and work their way home. As they were heading towards Carr's Hill they decided that it might be useful to put one up by the entrance to Mount Oval, as this was a large new residential area.

Putting up posters is a bit like riding a bicycle: it's a skill you never quite forget but it's also something that takes a bit of time to get back into the habit of again. You get stuck with the small things, like how far apart to space the poster poles, what type of nail head or screw to use, which way you put the cable tie to get the poster facing out. For John and Noel, when the first poster was being put out they were delighted with themselves. It felt great to be driving timber stakes into the ground and putting nails through my forehead. The lads always tell me that they never got any satisfaction driving a nail through the eyes or forehead on the posters but I'm not convinced about that. I should have done a count to see just how many were put up this way.

Having put the poster up, the lads jumped back into the car and headed off to Carrigaline. By this stage William had joined them and was waiting at the roundabout in Carrigaline. William is always called the quietest one of the Buttimers but he has a steely resolve and fierce determination. It was William who saved our bacon with the pole posters, as he proved great at making sure they were put up and was the most able guy I've seen at climbing up extension ladders. No height seemed too great for him.

William, an accountant by profession, is a very organised guy. When the lads pulled up he jumped out of his own car and took a poster out of the trailer. 'Okay, where's the crowbar and sledge hammer?' he asked. John and Noel replied that they were in the trailer. William looked again and said they weren't. John looked at Noel and Noel looked at John, asking each other at the same time, did you put them in? It transpired that in their excitement and euphoria at putting up their first poster they jumped into the car without tying down the posters or putting the gear back in the car. William had to go back and get it while John and Noel fell about the

The battle of the posters in North-Central: Noel O'Flynn and Kathleen Lynch.

Bertie goes walkabout in Cork.

A middle-of-the-road man.

Pat Rabbitte and friends at the Lough.

Four women candidates in Cork: Sarah Iremonger (Green Party), Deirdre Clune (Fine Gael), Kathleen Lynch (Labour), and Sandra McClellan (Sinn Féin).

Mícheál Martin casts his vote.

A delighted Michael McGrath (Fianna Fáil) in Carrigaline following his general election victory.

Dan Boyle was only narrowly defeated in what was one of the most competitive constituencies in the country. It's a tough time to have to do a media interview.

The PDs tried hard, but the election was a disaster for them.

Billy Kelleher (*left*), who topped the poll in Cork North-Central, is congratulated by Michael McGrath, who went on to take the second seat in South-Central.

place laughing. As a team we almost always managed to have a laugh and joke while still getting the job done. Of course there were other occasions when things were serious and there was no time for laughing.

Tuesday 1 May

Another sunny morning and we are in Well Road at 7:30 a.m to meet the drivers in the traffic. I am invited to speak to the students in Regina Mundi in Douglas this morning.

Afternoon canvass in Turner's Cross and night canvass in Thornbury and Diamond Hill, Monkstown.

I am angered at the state of our mental health system. Just today I met a mother and grandmother both worried about their respective sons. At another door one voter is worried about her son, who is suffering from depression and is having difficulty accessing services. I feel that young men and single men are becoming marginalised by society.

The incidence of child and adolescent mental health difficulties is increasing year on year because of improvements in diagnosis of conditions. There is now a greater understanding that conditions such as depression, anxiety, attention-deficit disorder and conduct disorder exist and can affect young children and adolescents.

As a secondary school teacher and a sports administrator I regularly meet young people who because of external pressures are vulnerable to the development of mental health difficulties. I strongly endorse and welcome the Fine Gael initiative of substantially increasing funding for this area and in particular for ring-fencing funding to provide a youth mental health initiative aimed at teachers and other adults who have frequent contact with young people to address child and adolescent intellectual disability services, and increase in-patient and out-patient facilities.

Additionally, the Department of Health and the Department of Education have a role to play in increasing public awareness of what is and is not a mental health need. In particular I am calling for less emphasis to be placed on the medical model of classification and treatment by medication. International best practice (US, UK, Australia, Sweden) suggests that mental health needs to be viewed from a holistic perspective, taking into account biological issues, psychological issues and social issues. This bio-psycho-social model allows for sensitive understanding of the pressures and difficulties that a young person faces and allows for empowerment of the young person to identify solutions to their difficulties.

Under a Fine Gael Government I will also demand that resources are invested in outreach community programmes to reduce the understated number of deaths each year from suicide. Suicide occurs at the end of a long road for a person and is rarely or ever a first-step solution. Again, international research shows that suicide is not primarily related to any specific condition but more to a feeling of hopelessness that there is no solution or remedy to the problem. Services need to be available in local communities on a 24/7 basis 52 weeks a year.

It is time to change the manner in which mental health services are designed and delivered. At the moment we have a medical model and that needs to change to one which is person-centred and which aims to empower a person to manage and cope with their own problems or issues rather than medication which dulls and masks the symptoms but which may not provide a cure.

Wednesday 2 May

At the Kinsale Road roundabout on another warm morning to canvass in the traffic. The early morning rises are great. You get to see people in a different light.

Afternoon canvass in Mahon and night canvass in Alderbrook, Curragh Woods.

Launch our new leaflet on the elderly. Michael Aherne is pleased, as he is included in picture with me on front of leaflet. Michael has been ever-present since February 2004, when we started canvassing for the locals. He is the first to ring about a funeral, to raise a local issue. If only we had more like him!

PRESS RELEASE ON THE ELDERLY

Protection of the elderly is an important issue which I feel we as a party should raise more. People feel raising the pension and other social welfare entitlements is enough; it's not. The needs and rights of senior citizens have been neglected for too long. The current non-contributory pension of €209.00 is €3.00 below the official indicator of poverty. We have also witnessed and read horrific accounts of what has happened in some of the nursing homes in the country e.g. Leas Cross.

Nobody should be afraid of reaching old age and specific measures need to be adopted to ensure that old age is indeed a golden age for our senior citizens. The old age pension should be index linked with inflation and brought above the threshold for official poverty.

There should be an expansion of the number of home help hours available so that older citizens can stay at home as long as possible. This will benefit the older person socially and psychologically as well as being economically cost effective for the State.

Standards of care consistent with international best practice need to be established, introduced and monitored with a name and shame policy for those who break them.

A Junior Minister with special responsibility for co-ordinating the State response to senior citizens should be established.

Thursday 3 May

Canvassing in the traffic this morning on Gregg Road by St Fin Barre's Cathedral on another lovely morning, talking to students and parents as they make their way to the nearby national and secondary schools.

Afternoon canvass in Blackrock Road and night canvass in Shanbally, Ringaskiddy and Monkstown.

FG's stamp duty move is being described as 'desperation politics from a desperate party . . . a deathbed conversion.' It may well be, but it could be the promise that works.

Vincent Browne interrupts the FF manifesto launch. 'The problem about this money that you got from Mícheál Wall is that it ain't credible that it was for the purpose of the renovation of a house,' Mr Browne told the Taoiseach.

Initially, Mr Browne was stopped by P. J. Mara, at which point he recalled twenty years ago when he claims journalists were obstructed from asking the former party leader Charles Haughey questions. It was like a scene out of 'The West Wing'.

'I hope Fianna Fáil has changed and we won't be obstructed in doing so now,' Mr Browne added.

Jesus, Vincent, get off the stage—let's talk about the issues, not Bertie. Or maybe we should and do a job on him for once and for all. Do we know the right approach? Do people care? I get mixed signals on the doors: some want him out, others don't care, and the rest support him 100 per cent.

Sunday Tribune political editor Kevin Rafter speaking on RTE said this was a 'really, really bad morning for Fianna Fáil.'

'First of all, they were doing a U-turn on stamp duty,' commented Mr Rafter. 'And then the Taoiseach was dogged again on the tribunals.' He added that even though Mr Ahern answered a question, the issues are still hanging over him. Yeah, but they are still being talked about.

Friday 4 May

At 7:30 this morning we are handing out leaflets to the traffic by Daly's shop in Douglas. Today is the day I hand in my nomination papers.

Message from FG HQ: party and Enda not commenting further on Ahern funds. 'Nothing further to say on the issue. Campaign should be about real issues like health, crime, etc.' Yes, but get the media to move and come out fighting on issues. We are allowing FF to sleepwalk and this whole saga is suiting them.

I don't buy this zone shit in FF election HQ, they are too cute. I see the way Shannon and the Martins operate. Christ, lads, they are playing with us: let's hit them on the issues.

At traffic lights this morning Derek says, get the page turned over to the day-to-day issues and we will have a chance. This money talk is a distraction.

We got some general advice from headquarters about how to dress for the official picture shoot. The night before was like a dress rehearsal in front of John, Rita and Noel. Trying to decide what tie to wear with which shirt and jacket was something I had very little interest in. Each of them had an opinion of their own. You need to look young, try to look serious, that's a real energetic-looking tie, breathe in, breathe out, smile, show your teeth and other comments were being flung about as if I wasn't there or had no feeling. In the end we agreed.

The official shots were taken with me standing, sitting, jacket on, jacket off, smiling, frowning, bored, happy, and about two months later I was sent a file of about twenty photos and was asked to select the ones I was most pleased with. If you've ever got married and had to compile a wedding album you could empathise with me over the decision I had to make.

As with many of the other decisions, this one went to the group. Selecting the appropriate picture is really important as it is used throughout the campaign, on different media, and is one of the main ways in which I, the candidate, would be projected. Thankfully the groups were pleased with the final outcome and chose a full-length shot and a close-up shot (a head and shoulders). This close-up shot was to become my main image and was replicated on all our election literature thereafter as well as being the key picture for the pole posters.

With the delay in getting our posters down to Cork the official campaign had started before they arrived. Having seen the mock-ups and a favourable response to the picture on the leaflets, I couldn't wait for the pole posters to go up. John went out to the depot to collect them and rang me in an agitated manner. I was with some people but he said he had to talk to me. John rarely made such demands and when he does it's usually for a good reason.

He said the pole posters were disastrous, awful, and he wasn't sure if we should use them. Knowing that John can sometimes be a perfectionist, I thought, okay, they might be bad but sure they can't be that bad. As it happens, they were truly awful. The pictures lacked any discerning features and were monochrome in appearance.

Thankfully, Simon's and Deirdre's posters came exactly the same way. Hurried phone calls to Ken and Dave McCarthy didn't elicit any further information or hope that the matter would be resolved quickly. It seems that the printers rushed the job and didn't put the posters through the final run. Running a campaign is bad enough without having to deal with stuff like this in the middle of it. It's okay to mess up the things that you are responsible for but it's very difficult to control your emotional response to things that are beyond your control and which are key and central to your plans.

We were given a choice by Ken and Dave. Put up or don't! I was told that there would be a new delivery of posters but that it might take a week to ten days to arrive. That was half way to polling day. My father, William, John and the rest of the team were going apoplectic with rage. The suggestion from Ken and Dave was put the posters up and when the new ones arrive replace them. As with many things in life, this was easier said that done.

I was relying on the generosity of William, Noel, Derek, JJ, Brendan, Peter and the others to put the posters up for me, and it was difficult enough to ask them to do it once: now I would have to do it a second time. Fortunately they were an obliging bunch and didn't complain to me, but I wouldn't blame them if they read me to their friends or families.

The pastel posters, as we called them, caused a bit of a stir. I suppose, looking back on it, no publicity is bad publicity. There was radio and print coverage of the posters and they featured in phone-ins and on opinion pieces in the local newspapers. Local reaction seemed to be split, with some people liking them and others thinking they were hideous. One or two people even thought it was a deliberate design feature and that the posters were done to resemble Japanese anime art. At least people were talking about us. The publicity attached to the posters also showed me how much work I still had to do in getting my name across in the general public and in being taken seriously as a candidate.

The local paper ran a piece on the posters and named Deirdre and Simon in the header, but there was no mention of me. I did feature in the article but often people only read the headlines. This was a wake-up call and showed that I needed to press ahead stronger than before with press releases and in getting my message heard.

Saturday 5 May

Afternoon canvass in Carrigaline.
First poll of the election is out today. It's very much game on: Fianna Fáil are at 37 per cent, down two points since September. Fine Gael are at 26 per cent, up two. Labour are at 13 per cent, up three. The Progressive Democrats are 2 per cent, down four. The Greens are at 6 per cent, unchanged. Sinn Féin are at 8 per cent, down one. Independents and others are at 9 per cent, up three.

John messages us all to say keep up the good work.

Response is good. I'm encouraged. Runaway Clune and Coveney? I don't think so. But who knows? The bottom line is we are getting a good response at the doors. I would hate to be a FF canvasser. Maybe they are not as impolite as they would suggest.

RTE On Line said, 'The figures reinforce three impressions about the election campaign.'

First, Fianna Fáil are facing an uphill battle to match its 1997 result, never mind 2002.

Second, that Fine Gael and Labour are mounting a very real challenge to the current Government.

And third, that for either of those alternatives to actually get into government they are very likely to need the support, whether inside or outside the Government, of the Greens, or Sinn Féin, or independents.

The end of the first week of campaigning in the general election has been marked by debate over Mr Ahern's personal affairs. Will they stay or will they go? The PDs are back in the news. McDowell is under pressure and is trying to stay relevant. Rumours are that they are on the verge of pulling out of Government. Well, Tánaiste, the people today are fed up of you and the PDs. Could this be the defining moment that allows people looking for change to make that happen and come across, or will it galvanise FF supporters? I wonder.

Sunday 6 May

This morning we go to the first Mass in Crosshaven. We then go on to Carrigaline and Ballygarvan to talk to the people as they come out of Mass. After lunch we go back to Crosshaven to canvass in what turns out to be a very wet day.

Noel Condon, Dad and myself are out in the rain. It's dirty and wet. Very few home but it has to be done. I hate doing Masses. I argue the toss with the lads. We did not do them in locals of 2004. William is like Schumacher as he drives from Crosshaven to Carrigaline to Ballygarvan. Ger Spillane and the others in the branch join us outside the gate. Councillor Lombard is in good spirits and we spent our free time taking the mick out of him.

But the main news is on Bertie and McDowell. 'This Week' is full of it. Speaking on RTE's 'This Week' programme, McDowell called on Mr Ahern to make a credible and comprehensive public statement on the issue. The PDs are saying no purpose would be served by them leaving Government and handing over the justice and health portfolios to people who are unfamiliar with the issues. Oh, please—now who's playing chicken; what happened to conviction politics?

Mr McDowell also said he would go back into Government with Fianna Fáil if a credible account was given by the Taoiseach and accepted by the Irish people.

I'm struck by his lack of a reply when asked if he had full confidence in the Taoiseach. He refused to directly respond. Have the PDs allowed themselves to be outplayed on this one?

We canvass in Carrigaline at night. McGrath will get some vote if all the people who promise vote for him.

Noel jokes: 'Maybe we should put money on him and defray the election costs!'

Monday 7 May

No 7:30 a.m. canvass this morning, as it's bank holiday. Night canvass in Carrigaline.

It must be stress setting in already. We had a huge team out in Carrigaline tonight—much larger than anticipated—so we were covering more estates than we had planned. At one point the group got split up and some, including myself, ended up spending about ten minutes walking until we found the rest of the crew. It acted as a reminder to never get too far away from the cars!

With a large team you can get a lot of houses canvassed in ten minutes, and every door knocked on really matters, especially as this is an area where I would not be that well known. It must have been the tension of being in the campaign itself that caused the bit of friction in the group—all over the ten minutes of downtime trying to locate where we were supposed to be! At the time I felt like we weren't organised or prepared enough and I let a few people know about it. To be fair to all the canvassers, everyone just kept on going and I think that they must have sensed it was all down to the stress of the campaign, even at this early stage. Sorry, guys.

FG manifesto launch. Enda launches our manifesto promising a wide range of taxation and spending proposals, including cuts in income tax and stamp duty and extra money for pensioners, and free medical cards for infants.

The question is, has Bertie distracted the momentum from us? I worry that people are focusing on Bertie and nothing else. It's all about the Poor Bertie syndrome. Sympathy for Bertie will win FF votes. Would the media ever let the story go? Why do they keep running it? Do we need it now? . . . Let the tribunal run its course. The ordinary person does not know or care about the details of Bertie's finances.

I launch my transport leaflet—we need to get Cork moving as I call for the immediate creation of a transport authority for the greater Cork area to resolve the traffic gridlock that is affecting much of Cork city.

We have canvassed close to 30,000 homes since receiving the nomination, and along with health, child care and education, traffic gridlock and congestion is the number 1 issue on the doorsteps.

People have told me—and I see it in the mornings —that it can take thirty minutes to travel one kilometre at peak times in the morning and evening. At off-peak the same journey might only take five minutes. During our canvass we have identified key black spots as the Rochestown Road, Douglas village, Donnybrook, Frankfield, Carrigaline and the Bandon Road and Sarsfield Road roundabouts.

To me it is clear from talking to people and reading council traffic surveys that bad planning and failure to invest in infrastructure has contributed to the problems experienced by thousands of Cork people every day. As well as affecting quality of life, traffic gridlock costs millions of euros each year in wasted working hours.

There is a need for greater resourcing of public transport: improved bus lanes, integrated and multi-journey ticketing. The current public transport system is not meeting the need for the current population and will not meet the projected demand going forward without substantial investment. People would use public transport and park-and-ride facilities if they were available, efficient and accessible.

Additionally, I feel greater emphasis should be placed on provision of a light rail system similar to Luas for Cork if the greater Cork area was to further develop. This, in conjunction with opening of closed railway lines to Midleton and possible new lines to Macroom and Ballincollig, would improve travelling options for daily commuters.

It's not just the Greens who can call for investment in public transport as an alternative to the car.

Tuesday 8 May

We are at the Carrigaline roundabout this morning. It is windy but dry. Afternoon canvass in Ballinlough Road and Boreenmanagh Road. Night canvass in Passage.

Main event of today is Stormont. The DUP leader, Ian Paisley, and Sinn Féin's Martin McGuinness take their pledge of office as First Minister and Deputy First Minister in a power-sharing administration. It's an extraordinary scene.

Who would have thought it? Miracles do happen. Delighted for the people of NI. Amazing how politics up there has changed and how FF U-turned from the Anglo-Irish agreement.

Today is not a day for politicisation of the North but you have to admire Bertie for the work he put in to the peace process. Of course Garret, Peter Barry and John Bruton deserve recognition.

William is all excited: Paddy Power has my odds at 5 to 4. Celtic Bookmakers have me at 10 to 1. In William's words, looking like a good bet. We chat about betting as we feel we are doing very well and in contention. It's a good bet and the odds are tempting.

William tests my bullish confidence: 'Well, I can get the lads into a syndicate and we can lash money on. That's not a problem.' I think aloud, worried—knowing William and his cronies—that this is not a €20 a head job. Why not, I say. Let's go, and if we win Ivan will be the poorer!

Wednesday 9 May

It is bitterly cold this morning as we stand on City Hall Bridge at 7:30 a.m. giving out leaflets. Canvass this morning in Roselawn and Edward Walsh Road. Afternoon canvass in Deanrock estate and night canvass in Woodbrook, Bishopscourt, Wilton Avenue and Merlyn Lawn in the rain. John in Brookfield Park and St Joseph's Park.

Meeting with sporting groups wanting to enhance participation of young girls in particular and I release a statement:

> **SPECIFIC STRATEGIES NEEDED TO INCREASE FEMALE PARTICIPATION IN SPORT**
> Cork has been lucky to have been well represented by extraordinary female athletes like Sonia O'Sullivan and the Cork Camogie teams.

However, that findings from recent national surveys on participation levels in sports and recreations, show that significantly less women participate in sport than men. Just under 40 per cent of women reported some participation compared to over 50 per cent for men ... I am calling for €5 million of National Lottery funding to be ring-fenced to promote and develop opportunities for women to become actively involved in sports and leisure activities.

Thursday 10 May

This morning we are at Trinity Bridge. Shortly after we arrive Simon Coveney comes along. He decides to go to Parliament Bridge. Evening canvass in Farranlea Park, Court Cairn, Highfield Lawn and Woodleigh Lawn. John in Tara Lawn, Hillside and Glendale estate.

MRBI poll today has us at our second-highest poll since 1999. The two Johns, as usual, urge caution and reinforce the message that we need to keep the work rate up. The election is there to be won. Enda, on 47, is up six, his highest rating in five years. I'm thrilled for him, as he is super; if only more people could see what he really is like.

Not the poll but the feeling at doors and at traffic lights. People are wanting to vote. It's as different as night and day from 2002. This time people are engaging and chatting about issues. Seriously looking at FG. Good man, Enda. Keep the big mo going, as the Yanks call it.

Friday 11 May

Our 7:30 a.m. canvass this morning is on Parliament Bridge. With a sore eye and the rain falling I head off on an afternoon canvass in Hartland's Avenue and the Lough. Night canvass in Uam Var estate, Chestnut Grove and Rossa Avenue. John and his team in Earlwood estate.

Met a woman today the victim of violence. Struck by her love and desire for her family and partner. I am appalled at her story. I promise to look into it. Analysis of domestic violence statistics suggests that evenings, weekends and special occasions e.g. Christmas show higher incidence rates.

I believe that lessons need to be learned from the many child abuse inquires that have taken place so as to ensure that the frequency and intensity of domestic violence is reduced. There needs to be an integrated response from all stakeholders, GP, Gardaí, accident and emergency centres.

Saturday 12 May

Enda Kenny was paying a visit to Cork that day and some of us had been invited to lunch at the Opera House and to take part in the walkabout of Cork city with him. This was going on at 1 p.m., so we headed out canvassing as early as possible—11 a.m.

Our block was contained to the South-East Ward for this few days, so we met at the florist shop at the Cross Douglas Road. We always had a number of teams out but on this morning it was raining and, it being Saturday morning, canvassers were not too keen. But they would be out in the afternoon and for the evening, which was the normal course of canvassing.

We started the day with about ten people, all set with our umbrellas and rain jackets, praying for the rain to die off for the leader's visit at least. Although it was raining it was still May and was fairly humid. So when you wrap up, thinking you're doing the right thing, although you're keeping yourself dry it tends to get exceptionally warm underneath the layers, especially when you're on the move.

Noel Cregan's role on the day was to track the electoral register, to ensure that we knew who we had at every house. This meant sticking with the candidate at every door and also co-ordinating the rest of the canvassing team to make sure that I knew where they were, and vice versa. Whenever a canvasser had somebody at a door, it was his job to make sure I made it to that door, and to tell me who they were, by looking at the register before we got to the door.

A few months ago this was not a problem, but when you have a large team knocking on doors, moving at a much faster pace, it's very difficult to keep track. We kept all the registers in the boot of my car, as we did with all the literature. Hence my car always became the focal meeting point for every canvass. We search the boot for the electoral registers that morning and, as it happens, the area we were covering this morning straddled a few different polling stations. This meant that one side of the road had a different electoral register from the other, so keeping track of the names of people in houses proved difficult. The electoral register sometimes has even numbers of houses on one page and has odd numbers on another, as in this case it did.

So Cross Douglas Road was divided between two registers, of which houses were listed on two pages in each. Trying to keep the registers dry with an umbrella overhead, and trying to read them by holding one in each hand while at the same time trying to manage the candidate on this particular day became very frustrating. It's the rain that spoils it. But Noel did really well.

It was our second time canvassing this area, and, thankfully for me, between Noel and me we remembered a lot of the people from the previous time we canvassed. Thankfully I am good at recognising faces and names (eventually) and can remember people I met some months ago for two or maybe three minutes. According to Noel, 'He would ask them how are they getting on working with, say, the taxi company, or if they were involved in a local club or society he would ask them about that. This impressed many people and made them feel as if Jerry knew them personally. He may not have known anything else about them but it was enough to get on people's sides. But he has a genuine interest in people and what they do, and this enables him to connect with people on their level very effectively.

'As a team we never waste time when canvassing, and in particular for the last few weeks I would be on Jerry's case not to stay too long at any one door. This was difficult because if I interrupt a conversation with a voter I'm considered rude and may risk losing the vote, if we ever had it in the first place. Some people who would be considered staunch supporters of another candidate may want you to stay talking for different reasons—to keep you there so that you won't make it to other people.

'On this day we happened to meet a member of our own party, who was supporting one of the other Fine Gael candidates. Once Jerry engaged in debate with him in the middle of the street I had to tell our friend where to go and get Jerry away from the situation without him losing his cool too much. The stress of the campaign can get to the candidate and it's important that he stay focused and listen to those that are on his side and not take notice of people that would like to sabotage our campaign.'

The weather dried up in time for the leader's visit, and the gang were able to don their 'Vote Jerry Buttimer' T-shirts for the leader's canvass. There were going to be reporters and cameras there, so it was important we were seen. Enda's agenda for the day was as follows:

1 p.m.—Lunch at Cork Opera House
2 p.m.—Walkabout Cork city
3:30 p.m.—Press conference Clarion Hotel
4:15 p.m.—Walkabout Douglas Court
5 p.m.—Walkabout Blackpool Shopping Centre
5:45—Walkabout at Ballyvolane Shopping Centre
6:45—Canvass at Grange-Frankfield church

As Blackpool and Ballyvolane are on the north side of the city, it wasn't necessary for us to go along there, but we would need to be seen at Grange church afterwards.

Enda Kenny's entourage arrived about 15 minutes before he did. A bus full of followers and staff and two green Nissan 4×4s swathed with Enda Kenny and Fine Gael illustration. Then Enda in his own car.

The weather had cleared and the sun penetrated through the clouds, which eventually moved east. Great, we had a nice afternoon for the walkabout.

A large crowd had gathered, anticipating the leader's arrival, and when he did he was welcomed by a rapturous applause of supporters, enticing other passing members of the public to stop and observe, most of whom were happy to see Enda in Cork and were able to shake hands with him and wish him the best of luck in his campaign. It was lunch in the Opera House, and we started our walkabout at 2 p.m.

We were greeted at the start by two or three far-left protesters, but Councillor Gerry Kelly was not to be outdone with his rendition of the 'The Banks', and the protesters couldn't be heard once everybody joined in with Councillor Kelly.

The walkabout was pre-planned, and Enda's handlers were ahead all the time directing the canvass. Keeping up with Enda was hard work. His energy and enthusiasm, however, became infectious and the followers were soon up to the beat of his stride. I was amazed at his vigour and oomph. He clearly has a huge appetite for what he does.

We made our way into Patrick Street, where we worked our way up towards Merchants' Quay shopping centre. On the way Enda and the general election candidates stopped to talk to people while the party stalwarts handed out literature to the public, while closely following the leading group.

I was proud of the team with their 'Vote Jerry Buttimer' T-shirt. I was doing my best to make myself visible. It was tough. Now I knew how the jockeys on the Grand National felt on the run to Beecher's! It's all about positioning, that picture, that one-in-a-million photo op.

Members of the team, John, Emma, Catriona and Marguerite were prominent in the background. Enda was able to connect with everybody he met on the walkabout and confidently engage in conversation on whatever topic came to pass, including listening to the concerns of a nurse met on the issue of the nurses' strike, which was ensuing at the time.

It was an issue that we had got at the doors a lot during the course of the campaign, and, as Noel kept telling me, 'Jerry was brilliant in empathising with nurses on the issue, as both his parents were nurses; he knew exactly what to say, but more importantly, he meant it. He was one of the genuine ones and people were able to recognise that.'

As we made our way into Merchants' Quay shopping centre somebody from the street fired an egg towards the leader. The aim was atrocious and the egg hit the wall above the door to the main entrance. At this stage Enda Kenny was inside the shopping centre but the remains of the egg did manage to drip down onto Bernard Allen's shoulder. He took off his jacket and moved on. No big deal. Good one, Bernard.

Through the shopping centre and out through the other side to Maylor Street and into Oliver Plunkett Street, where Enda and the crew stopped to listen to a man who was busking. Again the effervescent

Councillor Gerry Kelly managed to borrow the guitar from the busker and entertain the crowd with his own version of 'The Fields of Athenry', much to everybody's entertainment.

People who were going about their daily business stopped to listen to Gerry Kelly and this attracted a larger crowd once people realised that Enda Kenny was the focus of the walkabout. One man I saw across the road was with his girl-friend and was taking out his camera to take a photograph. 'It's Enda Kenny,' he said to his girl-friend. I could see he was a fan, so I approached him. 'Sure why don't ya go over and say hello?' I said.

'I couldn't,' he responded, hopeful that he could.

I put my arm around his shoulder and walked him across the road. 'C'mon, he'd be delighted to meet ya, boy,' I said. 'Enda, say hello to this fella there. Show me the camera there and I'll take a photo.'

He handed me the camera and I took the snap. Enda had a brief few words with him and shook his hand while posing for the photo. 'This guy is like the paparazzi,' commented Enda about me while I was taking the photo. Made the guy's day.

We moved on towards the Clarion Hotel, where Enda had a meeting and held a press conference outside afterwards. At this stage his handlers were organising the trip to Douglas Court. The format down there was much of the same. We did manage to run into Mícheál Martin, who was canvassing outside Dunne's Stores.

Brief pleasantries were exchanged between the men and we moved on into Dunne's Stores, where a backlog of people formed who wanted to meet the would-be Taoiseach. Enda managed to get around the shopping centre and shake hands with a couple of hundred people within half an hour, after which it was time to head to the north side of the city, and time for us to head back canvassing.

This would have been close to five o'clock, and we met the team back at the florist shop at Cross Douglas Road. They had, of course, worked their way down towards Douglas and canvassed a number of housing estates in the meantime. We had to stop at the shop to pick up refreshments for everybody. We decided to go up towards Ballinlough and canvass until the church times came about. As it happens, a funeral was taking place in Grange church, so Enda was diverted to Rochestown church instead.

We started at Bellair Park and worked our way to Knockrea Park in Ballinlough. Dan Ryan was maintaining the register this time, which I was happy about. We always canvassed in pairs. Noel on this occasion was paired off with my brother John, who was my campaign manager. It had been a long day and we were all tired.

Noel was trying to slip away to meet his girlfriend, Sarah, later on in the evening. She moved to

Ireland from Britain in March. I don't think she was aware that unless she came out canvassing with Team Buttimer then she'd hardly ever get to see her beloved. She did bring herself out some nights, which is a story for another day!

As our tired legs approached another door Noel mentioned to John that this is where the nuns live. 'No bother, sure don't they have a vote too?' he replied.

I knocked on the door, and one of the nuns answered, who I recognised because I also lived in the area, but I didn't know her name.

'Hello, sister,' said John. 'Sorry to disturb you, but we're just calling to say hello on behalf of Councillor Jerry Buttimer ahead of the election; we're hoping that you can give him his vote.'

'Hello, gentlemen,' she replied. A broad woman of middle age but who was very receptive and welcomed us in a manner that she was almost happy with the visit. Another nun was in the background, cleaning the dishes. She smiled out and said hello but she didn't come out. 'Which party are ye with now?'

'Fine Gael,' replied John. 'Is that good or bad?'

'Sure 'tis not bad anyhow; sure Enda Kenny is a great man. And tell me about Jerry,' she said.

'Well, first of all I'm his brother John, and this is Noel Cregan ...'

'Cregan—are you anything to Dino?'

'I am,' Noel said. 'I'm his youngest son.'

'Sure that's great. He's a lovely fella himself.'

Noel nodded approvingly. 'Sure I'm a local fella myself, sister, we just live up the road.'

'That's right, sure I see him around, and your mother too. Are they keeping well?'

'No fear of them,' he said.

John continued, 'You know Jerry is a school teacher, and he's been on the city council for the last three years, and he's been working very hard for the community. He'll be an excellent Dáil representative.'

'Of course he will,' said the sister. 'I hope he does well now, God bless him. Ye won't be bringing in the abortion, now, sure ye won't?'

'Absolutely not,' said John. 'Sure Jerry is against that; sure wasn't he in Maynooth himself for five years,' said John, hoping for an approving response.

'Ah, bless him.'

'Ye have a lovely home here, sister, and sure isn't it a lovely area?' I said, hoping to change the direction of the conversation to a more light-hearted one.

'Yes, we love it here, and sure we have our little chapel here and all,' she said as she opened a door just inside the hallway to reveal a church-like room behind it. I was afraid in case she was going to invite us in, but we managed to change the conversation.

'Isn't it a lovely evening, sister? Please God it will keep up for a few weeks,' John said.

'Ah, sure hopefully it will. Do ye want to go in and say a prayer?' she asked, or suggested.

At this point I was fit to do a runner. The vote didn't matter—I was going to lose it anyhow, cause I would break down laughing if I went in. I was already laughing at the inside at the thought of it.

'Sure we'll say a quick one,' said John.

Noel takes up the story. 'I couldn't say otherwise; all I could do is play along. It might not be so bad if I can keep my cool. I'm not a holy person—I believe in God and have faith but I don't pray regularly. This was hilarious as far as I was concerned. John stepped in the door and I was behind him. He stood just inside the door of the chapel, so I had to step in front of him to get in. Once he got out of the way, trying his best not to look at me, I saw a much older nun sitting at the back of the chapel, sitting there as if in a trance, all on her own, praying to the Lord.

'This woman must have been about ninety years old. She was a very slight lady, with a small face nearly covered by her habit. This was too much for me. I couldn't contain the laughter and I could sense John behind me wanting to laugh too. We were like children in a classroom trying to hide our laugh from the teacher. We lasted about thirty seconds, and John tapped me on the back. I let him go out first and he spoke to the nun for another moment, which helped me leave the chapel, hopefully without the nun noticing my laughter. I'm probably codding myself by saying that I think I got away with it, but I'll tell myself that anyway. Myself and John laughed for the rest of the evening. Not to mention that in an hour's time we were going to a church to canvass again.'

We arrived at Rochestown church, and the other two candidates in the constituency were already there, Simon Coveney and Deirdre Clune. Enda arrived shortly afterwards. On top of that, Mícheál Martin arrived to do some canvassing. We couldn't keep away from this fella today.

Once Mícheál's people saw Enda Kenny outside the church they made a few calls, and within a few minutes more supporters showed up to canvass with Mícheál.

We now had four general election candidates, as well as Enda Kenny, outside the church, on top of dozens of supporters, and apparently the parish priest didn't even approve of canvassing outside the church.

A few minutes later Ciarán Lynch arrived to meet and greet, also with a couple of supporters with him. It couldn't get more packed with candidates—not at least until Senator John Minihan's jeep pulled in. As soon as he saw the amount of candidates already there he drove back out again. He did the right thing. If there were five candidates at this church the chances were that he would have another church all to himself.

We shook hands with as many people as possible outside the church, but it was our presence that mattered. Once Mass is over, the canvass is over in ten minutes; people don't like to hang around. It was back knocking on doors with our team for the rest of the evening. We stayed out canvassing every evening until 9 p.m. On this occasion, however, it was 7:30 p.m. I was knackered.

Sunday 13 May

Did the Masses in Ballinlough this morning. Went to Éabha's birthday party, my niece who is five years old. Afternoon canvass in Beechwood Park, Belmont and Somerton. Night canvass in South Lodge, Lake Lawn and Ardmahon.

Red C for the *Sunday Business Post* shows a two-point drop in Fianna Fáil support, to 35 per cent. Fine Gael has gained three points since last week, to 29 per cent.

My dad met a woman who, like countless others, is frustrated and concerned at the lack of support and services available to people and families affected by autism. Her e-mail:

> Dear Jerry,
> Having spoke to your Dad this evening, who was canvassing for you at my front door. This is my story: My son Seán [name changed] has autism and ADHD, he also has a learning disability. He is an ex-pupil of CABAS and was mainstreamed in [school x] in [year y].

He is getting five hours' resource a week and has a full-time SNA.

He got five hours' home tuition for two and a half years which stopped Feb last year, when Mary Hanafin decided that KIDS IN FULL-TIME EDUCATION ARE NO LONGER TO GET HOME TUITION. I continue to fund this myself as my child NEEDS home tuition to help him.

Seán is in fourth class this year, he is just about surviving in his class. As his mother I am very unsure of his future, IF he survives the last two years in primary, where does his go for second level??? What kind of a future is ahead for Seán in this wealthy country of ours??

Autism is a pervasive developmental disorder that appears to be affecting an increasing number of children, particularly boys. There are a number of different theories accounting for this increase in autism, but most centre around a combination of biological and environmental events.

The issue of autism is one that affects not only the child but also has implications for the family in terms of education, socialisation and increased care demands.

From canvassing over the past six months I meet an average of two families affected by autism each night. While each individual case is different, there is commonality of experience, of difficulties accessing appropriate services, and doubt regarding the future.

The initial difficulty experienced by parents is getting a diagnosis of autism. Very often parents are aware that their child's development is slightly different from that of other children, but there is up to a two-year waiting list at the HSE Southern Region Autism Assessment Centre.

Monday 14 May

Morning canvass in Ballyphehane. Night canvass in Browningstown Park and Ardfallen estate.

Beaumont. Usually the complaint is that there isn't enough facilities for young people and that all they can do is hang around and annoy elderly neighbours. However, things were a bit different tonight.

When Cork was the 'European Capital of Culture' a series of concerts were held in a large marquee in the much-underused showgrounds; since then it has become an annual event. It provides a great focus for people of all ages; this year there will be acts ranging from Fifty Cent to Elton John, catering for all tastes.

Tonight I was at one door and the people were complaining about the marquee; they said that the noise was excessive—they are obviously within hearing distance—and that they have to put up with sound checks during the day before having to endure the crowds later in the night. The complaints then went on to the fact that there was alcohol being sold at the events.

While the grievances were clearly legitimate, it does show the fine balancing act that those in politics consider when deciding on issues that affect the community. We can't keep people fully satisfied all the time, and on occasions, no matter what decision is reached, some are bound to disagree.

Over the last few years the treatment of the elderly in nursing homes has been constantly in the news; my Fine Gael colleague Fergus O'Dowd must take a lot of the credit for pushing this issue. It is a given that those who can't look after themselves must be treated with respect and dignity; the changes which are being implemented should ensure that. But again, you can't satisfy everyone.

Tonight I met a person complaining about the increased regulation of the nursing home sector and how all of this is going to have an impact on the profits. This person did, unsurprisingly, admit to being 'involved' with nursing homes. Whatever about profit margins, the priority of society must be the welfare of the patient; everything else comes a distant second.

Met a lady who had the following conversation with me.

'Oh, hello. You're the Boy Buttimer.'

I smile and say I am.

'Well, I have my mind made up. I'm voting 1 for Deirdre, 2 for Simon and 3 for Dan Boyle. And I might give you 4.'

Why, I ask, would you not vote the FG ticket in full and then add on the alliance.

'Well, I'm voting for a Government. But I have a problem: outside my door rainwater pools, so I need you to fix it.'

At first I was writing in my notebook, but then, upon hearing that I was at 4, I ceased writing. Why ask me and you're not voting for me?

'Oh, they are all national politicians. Their job is to make legislation. You're the local boy.'

So I thank her and duly leave. Think it's fair to say that the gravel in the drive was covered in dust. Following day I asked Dan Buggy to do the job.

On day of polling the lady called me to thank me for fixing the pot-hole and said, 'You'll be glad to hear I gave you number 3.'

Morgan Stack, a colourful independent candidate, e-mails and challenges us all to a debate.

> Dear Cork South Central election candidate,
> A number of days ago I issued a debate challenge to the candidates in Cork South Central. You can view this challenge here:
>
> http://www.youtube.com/watch?v=J_-szBN2DjQ
>
> I am now seeking to establish what candidates are prepared to participate in such a debate.
> The format of the debate will be determined by the number of candidates who agree to participate.

If all candidates agree to participate then it is envisaged that there will be time only for one address of approximately 7 minutes per candidate.

If only half of the candidates participate then there will likely be time for opening and closing statements.

If you are willing to participate subject to any conditions please list these in your response.

It is envisaged that the debate will take place in Cork City this coming weekend Sat/Sun 19th/20th May.

Please also acknowledge receipt of this invitation and forward acceptance or rejection by 8pm Tues 15th May.

Your response or otherwise may be publicised.

Kind Regards,
Morgan Stack.
Independent Candidate.

I agree to his request. Why not? Let's have a debate. John and his team canvass in Ballyphehane tonight.

Tuesday 15 May

Afternoon canvass in Ballyphehane: Pearse Road, Kent Road, Connolly Road, MacDonagh Road.

Out canvassing with former Lord Mayor and senator Dino Cregan. As usual, the canvass is lively with him.

Met this lady. 'Dino, I've been waiting for you.'

'What's wrong, girl?'

'See my hedge, I need it cut.'

'No bother, girl. Jerry here, our candidate, will get it cut. He's a good man to get things done.' In a moment of recollection Dino asks: 'Mary, didn't I help you buy the house from the city council?'

'You did, Dino. But I bought the house, not the hedge.'

Got a text from Dave from Passage: 'You received your first preference vote today; my friend an army officer posted his vote earlier.'

Night canvass in Douglas Hall Lawn and Well Road. John in Curraheen estate.

One of the other challenges when out canvassing is what to do when you meet canvass teams from another political party. Do you plough on in spite of them and battle it out, trying to get to doors before them, or do you make a tactical decision and decide to head off somewhere else, where hopefully people haven't been called upon already that evening?

I suppose the rules of engagement aren't written down anywhere, but there is a general understanding that whoever has started an estate or road first gets to stay, but there is usually time for a social chat and exchange of views with the other teams.

Tonight we met a team out for John Minihan, the Progressive Democrat candidate. We had started the estate at opposite ends and when we came upon them we had a third of the estate left to do. It was the ground they had just covered, so we felt there was little value in knocking at the doors of people who had just been canvassed.

I hate moving, as it disrupts the overall canvass plan; something might happen to prevent you getting back to where you left and it wastes valuable time for canvassing and meeting people, as canvassers usually have to get into their cars, drive to the new meeting point and start the process all over again. The estates we were in tonight are large to medium-sized but are spaced well enough apart, so we really had to drive. However, some of the canvassers decided that they'd walk down and meet us. We got to the new estate and I started to canvass with the rest of the team, confident that Michael, Dan R. and Hugh would soon join us.

After half an hour John Coughlan got anxious and started to look for the three men. There was no sign of them. I had to allocate two people from my now diminishing team to find them, and to make matters even better it was starting to rain and we had to find shelter. For three-quarters of an hour John and Noel drove up and around estates looking for the three men, to no avail. As none of them had mobile phones, John rang Dan R.'s house, only to discover that they had gone home for a nice cup of tea while the rest of us had got soaked. They had gone to the wrong estate and when they felt the first drop of rain decided to head for the hills.

Wednesday 16 May

Afternoon canvass in Grange Park, Douglas. Night canvass in Maryborough Woods.

The Other Debate.

When the votes are counted on the 25th it is most likely that the smaller parties will be the ones that decide whether it is Fine Gael or Fianna Fáil leading the next Government, and tonight was the opportunity for their leaders to go head to head. The debate was bound to be a lively affair, with some very strong personalities and able debaters tackling one another in a fight for their political futures. Adams is seasoned in dealing with the issues of Northern Ireland, and he is Sinn Féin's biggest electoral asset, but how would he do on the real day-to-day political issues that have to be addressed in this forum? McDowell and Rabbitte are well known for their debating skills and should at the very least make it good viewing, but the real question was, how will Sargent do when up against the big boys?

As expected, McDowell dominated the hour. Whatever one thinks of his policies you have to give him credit for his ability to attack other parties and defend his own positions. He made it quite clear that for the PDs it's all about the economy, scare tactics and trying to get the voters to feel like they owe them, that the PDs must be thanked for the mess in the health service and the increase in gangland murders that have occurred whilst they have been in power! Somehow I think that the one thing that will be thrown away on 24 May is the PDs!

Pat Rabbitte was well able for what was thrown at him tonight. He knew where he wanted the debate to go and he stuck to hammering home his message. On the doorsteps there are concerns about Labour being in charge of the economy, and tonight Rabbitte was doing all he could to dispel these concerns by clearly stating that the only way change can be achieved is by maintaining economic progress. When attacking the Government he stuck to the PD ministries, as they are the ones that the voters are most annoyed about: health and crime—that's what people want to talk about.

The Greens must also know that their weakness is also the economy, as Sargent was at pains to point out that they would cut 'business taxes'. While this was there to reassure people, he always came back to the party's simple messages: climate change and cleaning up politics.

The debate really got interesting when Adams and McDowell went head to head. Adams is clearly not used to dealing with the run-of-the-mill political issues that were being discussed; he kept everything vague, and it was all about 'rights', the 'common good' and 'public money for public facilities', without ever getting into specifics. Whenever he could the debate went back to the peace process, all in an attempt to avoid the real issues, and this was like a red rag to a bull as far as McDowell was concerned. Everybody knows that all politicians have an agenda and that no matter what the question is they will somehow get back to talking about what they are interested in, but tonight Adams wasn't even trying to hide the fact that he didn't want to talk about the issues.

Surely when he said to Mark Little, 'The issue is what I want to talk about,' he must have realised that it was not his night and that he was being beaten off the pitch. The person doing most damage to Adams was McDowell; he is the one politician who can get at Adams; he's not frightened to have a go and he certainly doesn't hold back. The questions on affording a holiday home on an average industrial wage were priceless—and Adams had no come-back.

One-line put-downs in debates can either work really well or else they die a painful death, and tonight we got a few really good ones. You know what they say about the best one-liners being the ones that are most practised; well, I really think a lot of practising went in for tonight. McDowell's one about sitting among 'the left, the far left and the leftovers' was brilliant for its comical effect; however, Pat Rabbitte's description of McDowell as a 'menopausal Paris Hilton' was unexpected and definitely memorable.

Overall I think that McDowell probably came out on top tonight—well, from a purely debating viewpoint anyway—but I don't think it will do him any good next Thursday. Rabbitte also did well: he was reassuring and composed—a good night for the alternative. However, the abiding memory of the night was the poor performance of Gerry Adams. He clearly doesn't know about the political issues that matter, and the Sinn Féin electoral team must, for once, be regretting putting him up front for such an important occasion.

Thursday 17 May

Canvass in Grange Heights in the afternoon. Night canvass in Greenwood estate.

With a week to go it's the big debate. Enda v. Bertie.

Today's focus was all on the leaders' debate; for anybody interested in the election this is a must. For those of us running, tonight we saw the leader of our party holding our future in his hands. Surprisingly, over the last week the debate has been brought up on the doorsteps; clearly the voters still need to be convinced that the alternative Government is a safe option. With swings back to Fianna Fáil over the last few days tonight could have been decisive. I'm not sure if tonight is what it all comes down to—yes, people still need to be convinced, but these debates don't win elections, even if they have the potential to be a political banana skin. The aim for Enda was to show that he is competent, to reaffirm to people that he has what is needed to be Taoiseach. I am pleased that he did. Enda demonstrated his ability to debate, to lead, and I was happy with his performance.

I think that the debate was a victory for Bertie. There was a clear difference between himself and Enda, a difference that comes with the ten years' experience of being Taoiseach that he has. I don't think Fine Gael came out of it too badly; it was by no means a knockout, but it was definitely a victory on points.

Tonight highlighted a difference in approach between Fianna Fáil and Fine Gael in the campaign. The Taoiseach was ruthless; he was aggressive and didn't hold back, even when he was blatantly telling half-truths, particularly when he claimed that Breast Check was fully rolled out—try telling that to the women of the country on waiting lists for mammograms—whereas Enda was polite, he was a gentleman. That's all well and good on certain occasions but not when you are trying to win an election. The reserved approach that he took almost made him come across as if he was unsure of our policies, and those of us involved in the party know that is definitely not the case.

I was shocked when the issue of crime came up and Bertie threw the curve ball at Enda over the crime figures. In fairness to Enda, he has to rely to some extent on his front bench, and to be let down like that is disappointing; it brings to mind the game show hosted by Anne Robinson.

Overall, as I said, Bertie won but not by that much; Enda must now be seen as a credible candidate for Taoiseach. Tonight he was competent; he wasn't beaten out the door by a man who has been there for ten years.

RTE's late-night analysis was very interesting. I am somewhat surprised to hear the commentators calling it a draw; we'll take that as the verdict.

Friday 18 May

Night canvass in Willow Park, South Douglas Road.

Day after debate. Views mixed but by and large people felt Enda did okay and was not knocked out. That's good. Crime figures let us down. Good one, Jim. The media could have gone to town on us but they haven't; I really am convinced that they either want us to win or else they are doing all that they can to make sure this contest goes right down to the wire.

I liked Enda's remarks as he asks, 'Do I look as if I'm marked?'

Saturday 19 May

Canvass in Westgate, Ballinas Lawn, Firgrove. 'I would love to give you the number 1, but I'm voting for a Government.' 'I have to support FF. I don't know can I trust you, Labour and the Greens. I don't think you have the experience to manage the economy.' These were some of the comments being passed at traffic lights and canvassing today. There is a move afoot; now people are afraid to change ...

The PD poster 'Left-wing government' is noticeable on the poles in Bishopstown. They have made a decision to court the middle class through fear. I wonder will it have an effect. Dad looks at me coming out of the house of a well-known GAA activist in the club and matter-of-factly says he will not give you number 1. I protest, and Dad says he didn't look you in the eye. Point taken, I reply ...

Just as we finish canvassing, word comes out of a new poll which shows support for FF on the increase, while both we and Labour have slipped in the past week. 11 per cent of people are still undecided according to the Millward Brown-IMS poll for the *Sunday Independent*, which we feel is low.

After canvassing we stop for food in McCarthy's bar on Model Farm Road. We chat, review the day's events and look forward to Masses tomorrow. The mood is upbeat and the crew are in good spirits, with nobody safe from the tongue of John or Siobhán. I am particularly delighted that Michael Aherne has stayed with us. He is older than the rest but brings a breath of wit and enthusiasm to the canvass.

Sunday 20 May

Four days to voting.

Canvass at the Masses in Bishopstown. Afternoon canvass in MacCurtain Villas. That night the news of the *Irish Times* poll comes out: we are down and FF are up by 5. The rain does not help and the mood is sombre. We finish and head to the rendezvous for a drink and dry-off. Is it worth it? Noel and John recognise that there is a change afoot.

Privately we stop and have a quick chat. The middle-class voters are not voting for change. They are going to stay with FF. We all agree.

I contend that this is imperative to us and to our vote in the South-West Ward. John and Noel feel it could affect the other two candidates more. Still, it's into the end game now, just two days of campaigning left.

I go home despondent, fearful that the tide is going against us but hopeful that our message, our campaign and our work load will carry us through.

For the first time ever I didn't bother to watch 'The Week in Politics'. I just couldn't.

Text sent out by Enda lifts morale, and all the troops are thrilled to read it. 'Friends, we have four days left before winning this election. Every poll since this campaign began shows the alliance for change on course for victory. Keep up the hard work. Enda K.'

The leaflets, posters and door-to-door canvassing are the most public and visible aspects of any political campaign. As a candidate I am very involved in the design of these but have to delegate and rely on my team and supporters to actually bring them to fruition. To the casual observer, posters appear overnight and there is very often little or no consideration given to who puts them up, where they are put up, in what density and even at what height. These are issues that have consumed my strategy group for weeks.

I have often heard that posters don't work and why are they put up at all. As a new candidate, posters were extremely important for me as it is one of the most cost-effective ways to get both name and picture recognition in geographical areas outside what would be considered my home base. Making sure the posters remained intact and in situ during the campaign fell to John, William and my father. Every night following canvassing, John and my father would sit into a car around ten o'clock and take a drive around the city and the constituency. Each day we frequently received calls from concerned residents or friends about vandalised posters (usually the more expensive eight foot by four posters or the six foot by four posters), half hanging-down pole posters or areas where our supporters felt there should have been posters but there were none. Friday, Saturday and Sunday nights were particularly busy nights, as people going home from the pub or with the excess of the week seemed to get great satisfaction from targeting election posters. As a candidate you get paranoid that it's only yours that are being targeted, but I'm reassured by my colleagues on all sides of the political divide that everyone's posters were targeted equally.

On the final Sunday of the campaign, John and Dan were out on one of their nocturnal excursions, fixing and replacing posters and putting up some of our new four by four text posters. I only heard of this escapade on the night polling closed, as the team supporting me felt that if I was told I'd have lost the head and may have done something which I would later regret. This is where the importance of having a strong team behind you counts. It is important not to have a group of yes-people but people who are supportive, show initiative and who can make decisions. Within our group we always tried to arrive at decisions on a consensus basis, and this we did, but frequently after heated and frank debate and exchange of ideas. The reality is that while the candidate is involved in most decisions, there are many things which are kept back from the candidate for a variety of reasons.

Anyway, getting back to the night in question, John and Dan had set off about 11:30 p.m. to fix posters. This was particularly important, as the Bishopstown area had been poster-blitzed by Mícheál Martin and John Dennehy of Fianna Fáil as well as by my own colleague Deirdre Clune. The night before John had counted 68 Clune diamond posters on three local roads, covering approximately two miles. I found this level of intensive postering in my home patch as a personal attack, but in retrospect I have to admit it was an effective use of posters by the Clune camp; and the density of postering did cause comment locally. John had made calls to Ken Whyte, director of elections, querying the validity of the quantity of posters put up, but he was informed that as there was no divide and Deirdre had not broken her share of proportional distribution of posters there was nothing he or I could do about it. To counter this onslaught John decided that we needed to move some of our posters and to change our own distribution pattern to try and counter some of these attacks.

Around midnight, as John and Dan were attaching a poster to the roundabout at the CIT on Model Farm Road, John received a phone call from a high-ranking member of the Clune camp. Having a good relationship with this person prior to the campaign,

John was not surprised to get a call, even at this late hour. During campaigns, candidates and their teams are always on duty, and phone calls up to midnight are the norm rather than unusual. Normally these conversations are like games of chess—polite and diplomatic until such time as the real reason for the call or contact is revealed. However, John quickly realised that this conversation was not going to fall within the commonplace, as the tone and language immediately became antagonistic.

In between the threats and abusive language John's heart began to sink and his mind was racing. At the time he wondered was this the beginning of the end. We were accused of having carried out an unauthorised leaflet drop outside our agreed zone for that three-day block. Immediately John was extremely worried, as the implications of doing an unauthorised drop were extremely serious. The director of elections could have issued a counter-leaflet, which could have placed me in an awkward and embarrassing position publicly and within the party, but more worryingly the infringed-upon camps could have demanded and, more than likely, have got permission to put out a leaflet of their own in that area or, worse, in mine to which I would have had no right of reply.

Even though only John and I had access to election material, Dan said John's initial tone was one of caution, with a hint of fear and anxiety. John tried to remain calm but Dan said you could see the adrenalin beginning to pump through his veins. John asked a series of questions—the standard ones any reporter might have asked: what was dropped, where was it dropped, when was it dropped, who found it, who dropped it. As the answers to these questions were revealed, Dan and John immediately began to relax, as John knew that it was impossible for him or his team to have dropped the leaflet.

The lads were told that our official canvass card had been dropped and that there were hundreds of them floating around Ballinlough. At this stage John was certain that no drop had taken place, as there would have been no tangible benefit to dropping the canvass card, as all three candidates were on it and with the back of the card given over exclusively to Enda Kenny, Deirdre Clune and Simon Coveney. Our other literature followed the guidelines laid down by the director of elections: 80 per cent on me and 20 per cent given over to the Fine Gael team.

Despite trying to reassure the other person the accusations kept flying. The tone and language of the phone call was hot and heavy, with accusations and counter-accusations flying. During the call, John was accused of having been seen personally dropping leaflets into houses and that a number of people had seen him do it. Again John knew that he had the upper hand, as that very evening, while he was supposedly dropping the unauthorised leaflet, John had arranged thirty people into three canvass teams, had led a team of ten people canvassing Bishopstown and had arranged to meet the director of elections earlier that evening. Throughout the day John had been in the company of people who could vouch for his movements, and tried to get this across. Still the accusations were flying and threats were made for us to keep out of the South-East Ward, and that the Clune camp had ten thousand leaflets to flood Bishopstown.

This was the final straw for John. Raising his voice, he asked the other person to withdraw the charge they had made in relation to him having being seen personally dropping the leaflet. Eventually, tiring of the call, John calmly asked the other person to put the allegations in writing, with the names of those who had allegedly seen him making the drop in writing, to his solicitor. Dan said there was something surreal about this series of allegation and counter-allegation culminating in the threat of litigation for slander.

However, the evening didn't finish there. After the phone call both John and Dan were pumped. They had a mini war council in the middle of the CIT roundabout on Melbourne Road, and anyone passing must have wondered at the unusual sight of two grown men pacing around a small roundabout. How the Gardaí weren't called then or later I can't understand, as I've often received calls from concerned residents about less at later times in the night. John and Dan replayed the conversation and agreed that it was extremely serious and that some action needed to be taken. They agreed not to call me or Deirdre Clune, as one of the unwritten rules is that the strategy teams try to sort things out and leave the candidates neutral or as uninvolved as possible. The only course of action was to ring Ken Whyte, director of elections, inform him of the allegation and issue a full statement of denial.

My team had had regular contact with Ken over the past couple of days, and a call even at this late hour was not unusual. There was so much contact between John and Ken that John had Ken's number on speed-dial. As can be imagined, Ken was only too delighted to take the call and took the matter seriously. He took John's assertions of innocence for what they were but said that he would have to do some further investigations. As only Ken can, he warned John that if he found out the allegations were correct there would be a heavy price to pay. Again John protested his innocence. Within ten minutes Ken rang John back and said that from his perspective he had heard two different stories and both sides equally adamant that they were right. How was he to decide between the two?

Ken, originally from the Bishopstown area, had moved out of the city a couple of years previously and lived almost ten miles outside the city. Extremely annoyed and almost angry, he said that the only course of option to him was to go to Ballinlough and to see the evidence for himself. John and Dan were okay with this but demanded that if Ken was going then they too should also be present. An arrangement was made whereby Ken, John and Dan would meet a member of the Clune team outside Ballinlough church at 1 a.m. and the matter would be resolved then.

Being closer to Ballinlough church than Ken, John and Dan pulled up outside the church, where the Clune person was standing waiting for them. Despite having William's estate car, they were unable to offer her a seat, as the car was laden with posters, cable ties, a step ladder, crowbar, sledge hammer, two claw hammers and an assortment of screwdrivers, nails and screws—everything needed for a busy night of poster repair. In keeping with the surreal nature of the rendezvous, no mention was made of the reason for the meeting, and a pleasant ten minutes were spent chatting about the weather and general chit-chat about the social scene in Cork.

Eventually Ken arrived and he, John and C. stood in the Ballinlough church car park, within the shadow of the grotto, and tried to make sense of why they were there. C. was adamant that when she returned home from canvass she found a Buttimer canvass card on the floor. Perturbed by this, and fearing something more sinister, she went for a walk around Ballinlough around half nine, to discover that our canvass cards were everywhere. John flatly rejected this. As neither side backed down, Ken said that the only thing to do would be to walk around Ballinlough to see if evidence of the drop could be found.

With this the trio set off up the Ballinlough Road and started to go into houses with porches and visible hall floors. John was raging at this stage, as he knew the allegation was a total fallacy, but the charade had to be carried out. Turning right off the Ballinlough Road, they searched every possible house for any visible signs of leaflets. The weather in May was seasonably warm and dry, and John thought that in other circum-stances this would have been a pleasurable experience, and the clear sky and heavy scent of garden flowers pervaded his memory.

For over an hour the trio marched around Ballinlough and the estates, down onto Boreenmanagh Road. Along the way, leaflets from other candidates were found, including Dan Boyle of the Greens, Ciarán Lynch of Labour, Mícheál Martin of Fianna Fáil and a Deirdre Clune leaflet. In a couple of houses that were clearly rented a Buttimer leaflet was found, but one of these predated the calling of the election, and the quantity of uncollected literature made it abundantly clear that these leaflets were dropped weeks if not months previously. John's ire was raised to boiling point at this stage and at one point he threatened to knock on the doors of housing to ask if Buttimer leaflets had been dropped that day or not. Thankfully, Ken managed to persuade him that that might not be the most prudent course of action to take. How they were not spotted or reported for attempting to break and enter I'll never know.

After an hour John was starting to get more confident and bullish and eventually Ken conceded that the escapade and adventure would have to end. Being the diplomat, Ken refused to make a judgement there and then on whether there had been a drop done that night or not, but he was inclined to agree with John that no such drop had taken place. John's reasoning was that if we had done a drop then leaflets should have been found in houses where a drop by another candidate was clearly evident; in particular, Dan Boyle seemed to have carried out such a drop.

Arriving back at the church car park, the three again had words, with Ken promising to respond on the matter the following morning. Close to exhaustion, John walked back to the car to find Dan awake and alert waiting for news. John dropped Dan home and retuned to try and catch some sleep for himself.

Both Dan and John were present for duty at the roundabouts the following morning at half past seven, and neither mentioned the events of the night before but made some passing references to it being a pleasant evening for a stroll. As I said earlier, I never knew about this until the night of polling and I firmly believe that Deirdre was never informed either.

Monday 21 May

Had a meeting with the lads; we were talking about the early morning canvasses and someone said that he noticed too many people were eating junk food on their way to work and school, and even though he understood that they were under pressure for time etc. I said we should do something to try to encourage people to eat more healthily, especially at breakfast time.

We discussed this for a while and came up with the idea of handing out a healthy food option the next morning, when he was going to be outside St Columba's School in Douglas.

Derek and Paula set about putting together 150 pieces of fruit (50 apples, 50 bananas and 50 oranges), 150 bottles of water together with Jerry's health leaflet into snack bags and have them ready for the following morning. I was able to source the quantities that we needed as well as the bags to contain them, and after dinner that evening Paula and I set up a little production line on the kitchen table, putting everything together. Even my two boys, Robert and Oliver, got involved, helping out and signing 'Number 1 for Jerry' every time we filled a bag.

The following morning John, Jerry, Rita, Noel, Catriona and I met at 8 a.m. outside Daly's supermarket. We were a bit apprehensive about the type of reaction we would get, considering this was something that was not done before. We needn't have worried! As soon as the traffic started to build up and the youngsters started to arrive for school, the packs went like hot cakes (pardon the pun)!

We got a great reaction to it, so much so that it was decided to repeat it again the next week, but this time we would do it in two different locations and twice as many bags!

Paula and Noel's girl-friend, Sarah, volunteered to assemble the bags this time, to which they reacted with much enthusiasm! Noel and I had promised to help out as soon as we came back from canvassing, but unfortunately we arrived home just too late.

That morning we set up at the Sarsfield Road and also at the end of the Airport Hill. Again we got a great reaction; if we had double the amount of bags, or if John stopped eating, we would have been able to distribute them.

My philosophy is about making a difference, making people think and having an impact. In a light-humoured sort of way I think we did that with this approach.

Brian Cowen attacked Enda Kenny's Contract with the People and said the Government had 'pricked the balloon' and there was nothing there but a bag of wind.

On 'Questions and Answers' he was on fire as he made short change of Coveney and the others. It's the economy, stupid. People are afraid of change.

They trust FF and are reluctant about the leap to us. We should have put a bruiser on 'Q and A'. This was the time for a Bruton, Hogan or even a Charlie Flanagan. It's a pity we lost so many of our heavy hitters in 2002.

Cowen was impressive on 'Q and A'. I watched with Dino, and both of us were shouting at the TV. Easy to do in the sitting room, but Jesus, lads, with it game on and entering the last five minutes you bring on your key players to hold possession and play out the clock. Playing for a win is one thing. It's not the time to introduce a gentleman. Oh, man, sorry, Simon, I'm fond of you but you're not a bruiser.

Trends confirmed by *Irish Times* poll.

The TNS-MRBI poll shows Fianna Fáil support up five to 41 per cent since the last comparable poll; the Progressive Democrats are unchanged at 2 per cent. We are down one to 27 per cent; Labour is down three at 10 per cent, while the Green Party is up one at 6 per cent. Sinn Féin is down one at 9 per cent and Independents and others are down one at 5 per cent.

Tuesday 22 May

Met a neighbour coming out of the post office. Proudly she tells me, 'I've just sent my vote off in the post. I voted by post, you know. Looked after you very well.'

For a moment I was thrilled that I had secured a number 1.

'I gave you number 2.'

'Oh,' says I. 'Why?'

'Well, who would do my jobs in the city council if you got elected to the Dáil?'

Despondent, I decided there was no point in arguing.

Peter Kelly's leaflets dominate today's campaign.

Now living in New Zealand, Peter Kelly is a former Fine Gael councillor on Cork County Council for the Carrigaline electoral area but more specifically for the Rochestown-Grange-Frankfield sweep of that area. Initially a member of the PDs, Peter joined Fine Gael at the request of Simon Coveney and we quickly became colleagues and friends. When I was director of elections for Fine Gael in the 2002 general election Peter was a leading member of my strategy group and he was a great sounding-board when I contested my first election for Cork City Council in 2004.

Peter was a very astute politician who was always the first to identify new means of connecting with the electorate. He was one of the first politicians in Cork to put out frequent newsletters, start political data-bases, query by e-mail, and was always using innovative print and design techniques.

In 2006 Peter decided that he and his partner, Nick, would try and establish a new life in New Zealand. Peter was unfortunate to have been caught in the squeeze between Deirdre and Simon, as his heartland was dead centre between theirs. Peter knew that if Fine Gael were to run a third candidate in the 2007 general election the party would have favoured either myself from the South-West Ward or Derry Canty from Ballincollig. When the Electoral Commission changed the constituency boundaries and Ballincollig was heaved off to Cork North-West, I was the main runner for the third slot. Even to this day I lament the loss of Ballincollig to Cork North-West, as I felt that I could have won a seat with Ballincollig remaining in Cork South-Central. Maybe Derry would have won the nomination. I don't know. Derry Canty is a great local politician and I would not have fancied taking him on at convention.

My sister and I teach in Ballincollig; my brother William is married in Ballincollig; his mother-in-law taught for almost twenty years in the local primary school; and many of my friends from Bishopstown have bought homes in Ballincollig. As they say in property circles, it's about location, location, location; in politics it could be equally said it's about contacts, contacts, contacts.

Despite the fact that Peter and I could have been political adversaries we became good friends. Throughout the campaign I was in regular e-mail contact with Peter and kept him up to date on the progress or otherwise of the campaign.

During our earlier strategy meetings we discussed the issue of getting endorsements from various colleagues on Cork City Council and Cork County Council. I was confident of securing public endorsements from my ward colleague Brian Bermingham and my long-time friend and mentor Denis 'Dino' Cregan, who was a councillor for the South-Central Ward for Cork City Council. Councillor Jim Corr and I have a very close working relationship, and he's a man I admire and respect and was hoping that he might issue a letter or leaflet on my behalf, but in the end the group decided not to ask him, as to do so might have placed him in an invidious position, as he was a ward colleague of Deirdre Clune's. In the county areas Simon had secured endorsements from Tim Lombard and John Collins, which my team had expected from the outset. However, this was okay, as we had great support from Tim's sister Siobhán and his family, and John Collins had given us a number of days' canvassing in Carrigaline. But there was still the unresolved issue of the endorsement from Peter Kelly.

Peter had e-mailed me about a month previously and stated that he would like to issue a leaflet on my behalf. The team was uncertain as to whether to drop the leaflet or not, as Peter had resigned mid-term and was not a public representative. I e-mailed Peter and told him the group was unsure but thanked him nonetheless. Peter, as the consummate politician, said that he would still like to do something on my behalf and suggested that he would write to his supporters, friends, former neighbours and contacts on his mailing list. This was as much as I could have hoped for. I agreed.

On the night in question, a number of us were gathered in my house sorting out a letter mail merge to people we had met during the campaign. Close to ten o'clock John got an irate phone call from Ken Whyte demanding to know what the hell was happening. John put the call on speaker phone so that John C., Noel Cregan and I, who had decamped to the kitchen, could listen to the call.

Ken stated that there was an illegal leaflet being circulated in Grange purporting to be from Peter Kelly and that as Ken had no prior knowledge of it and hadn't sanctioned it it had better be stopped. John denied knowledge of the leaflet but Ken wasn't buying this and demanded that John find out what was happening and put a stop to it straight away or else sanctions would be applied.

Again we were being accused of something in which we had no involvement or knowledge of. This event had to be viewed in the context of the alleged leaflet drop in Ballinlough, a difficulty we had encountered over canvas areas and the poster-blitzing of Bishopstown. We were beginning to feel under siege and as if the whole world was against us. Of course what had annoyed Ken as well as Clune and Coveney was that Peter Kelly did not inform anyone that he was giving me an endorsement.

As with most crises in the campaign, they happen late at night, but undeterred I rang Derek and asked him what was happening. He said that Peter had forwarded him two boxes of leaflets from New Zealand with a list of instructions about where and when to distribute them. It seems Peter had followed through on his endorsement after all.

We decided to finish the mail merge, as this was an important part of our strategy. By about 1 a.m. the letters had been printed, envelopes stuffed and stamped and the six or seven boxes were placed in John's car so that he and John C. could bring them down to the sorting office in Little Island to ensure they were received by Tuesday or the day before polling at the latest.

En route to the sorting office, John decided that it was the opportune time to ring Ken. Annoyed, Ken wondered if we ever slept or if we would ever let him sleep. John C.'s and John B.'s account of that phone call are interesting in their similarity but also in the discrepancies between them. At least they both concurred that it took place. Like many things, our recall of events is determined by our own perception of ourselves and how we like others to view us.

John stated that he remained calm throughout the call, but John C. suggested that he got quite emotional and at one stage he was shouting down the line at Ken. John was only too happy to inform Ken that there was a leaflet, that it came from Peter Kelly, that it was posted from New Zealand, and that Derek had directions on how to distribute the leaflet. For once Ken was speechless. But rightly so Ken was still dubious and demanded to see the leaflet, the box in which it was posted and the postal docket. Like an errant schoolboy, John agreed to meet Ken in the city the following morning and to show him the boxes and the leaflets.

The following morning John and Ken met on White Street, where John physically showed evidence of the literature. Ken commented that he had to consider what to do next in light of this turn of events. John made no further comment but got into his car and returned to join me and the others for the morning canvas. A little while later, about 12 noon, John got a call from Ken. A small victory for us, Ken was sanctioning the leaflet as he had to acknowledge that we had a real endorsement from Peter Kelly. His only stipulation was that we would have to overprint it with his name as the director of elections to make it compliant with the legislation governing the running of elections. Thankfully, having our own printer made this possible, and by 5 p.m. that day we had an official leaflet. The following day, John organised two teams to leaflet-drop the priority estates in Grange and Frankfield.

Wednesday 23 May

Thirty volunteers turn up for a leaflet drop in the South-West Ward. Dad, Dan and I canvass the local convents.

Met an interesting guy over breakfast in Douglas; here is his blog.

An undecided voter struggles to decide

I met Jerry Buttimer (FG candidate for Cork South Central) this morning.

In Douglas Shopping Centre, the Olive Tree café, where I was taking coffee with my good friend Garry after leaving Grace to her crèche …

A be-suited man, in a power tie, flanked by a minder who wore a tee-shirt urging 'Vote Buttimer Number 1', arrived for breakfast.

He was going off-duty. He looked tired (a good sign that he's been working hard), so I called him over. He's a lot shorter than I imagined. I probably think of politicians as colossi striding about on long legs (from which they often fall hard).

I told him we were both undecided.

He was up-front about looking for both our votes. And it turned out Garry has a grá for the Green guy, which I didn't know about (so that was good to find out). I remained unprepared to commit myself.

I showed him the photo of his leader, Enda, on the Irish Times today. I contrasted it with the rather triumphalism photo (the out-stretched arms one) that appeared a few days ago—the one that reminded me of Neil Kinnock's disastrous pre-mature celebratory photo. Jerry Buttimer had no interest in his leader. He was after our votes, and not after a waffling discussion about how political leaders project themselves. I admired his focus. I had something he wanted and I intended to make him work for it.

'So what do you think of that John McCarthy guy (who is standing in Cork North Central)?

'Ah, he's a good guy. Good ideas and articulate. I think we need to improve mental health services. Especially for young people, young men ... I think this is an important area ...'

The politician had no clue what I thought of John McCarthy's independent campaign for better mental health services. For all he know, I might have detested McCarthy, an auctioneer. I might have had no time for mentally ill people ... But he said what he thought, and didn't check out what I thought first. I admired that. He felt a bit more real than a normal politician (who first finds out what you think and then panders to it—that's what Deirdre Clune, FG, did when she came to my house ages ago).

I still don't know who I'll vote for. There is time yet for me to be persuaded.

Now, if FF are reading their Cork Blogs, and pick this up, I'd welcome a visit from your most hungry candidate.

Nurses have voted in favour of accepting proposals to end their work-to-rule. The result of the ballot of more than 35,000 members of the Irish Nurses' Organisation was 54 per cent in favour and 46 per cent against. So what did they receive, and why now on eve of polling?

Thursday 24 May

Election day.
Barry Keane sends out a message: 'Believe and it will happen.' If only it were that easy!

This is it. Last day. People on way to polls. We're on South Gate Bridge, immensely happy that we have reached the last day. Conscious that it's now in the hands of the people, I ask the people walking to work to vote to support me and to thank them for their courtesy.

'Come here, boy, are ye allowed do this? What happened the moratorium?'

I try to explain, but—

'Yeah, boy, it's the same, ye can make up and change the rules as ye like. We're tired of this.'

John and team do a 6 a.m leaflet drop in Rossbrook estate and Tramore Road.

John was responsible for many things during the course of the campaign. Some of these things are essential and some are downright stupid, but they all have to be done. Management of and organisation of the canvassers and canvass teams fell to John and my father. Ideally you'd like to have the schedules determined a week in advance but usually they were only finalised on the day itself. This led to the occasional bit of tension between John and my father but they were usually able to work it out.

In general we had a well-organised canvass, as we had identified areas that we wanted to focus on well in advance of the election being called. In addition, the constituency management system introduced by Ken made it easier again to narrow down where we might be. However, weather, other candidates and unforeseen events occasionally threw us off schedule.

One of the other things that gave rise to some management difficulty was the organisation of canvassers. As a long-time canvasser myself I truly appreciate the sacrifice that my friends and colleagues made in coming out canvassing with me. Some were only able to give one night during the campaign, others one or two nights a week, and for some they were out with me five, six and even seven nights a week and sometimes two or three times in a day. Each person gave what they were able, and while

John may have pushed for a little more I hope they really know how much they were valued and appreciated. As a candidate sometimes you might forget to say thank you at the end of a night or you might get a bit tetchy if things haven't gone right, but you do realise that without these people you're going absolutely nowhere.

Canvassers are an essential part of any election campaign, as it is close to impossible for a candidate to call to every house or to meet every person within a four-week period. In Cork South-Central the valid poll on election day was something like 90,000. Where would you be going? To derive maximum benefit from the canvassers that were available we would often split up into different groups.

I rarely saw John or my father on canvass evenings, as they were often leading groups, but we were in touch via text message as the need arose. Like any team, the canvass team is made up of individuals who are motivated to come out for different reasons and who have different personalities and needs. Thankfully, as a clinical psychologist John was more sensitive to some of these issues than I was and was able to avert some crises along the way.

I had no hand, act or part in who was assigned to me on any night, with the exception of Dan Ryan or Noel Cregan. Dan and Noel were essential for me, as they were personal friends from outside politics and politically they were two of the most experienced guys you could hope to find. Both had come up from the political school of hard knocks and were used to running a canvass team on the ground. In addition they were both able to read and work off the electoral register and had a working knowledge of Fine Gael policy. As key members of the strategy team they were also *au fait* with what the targets were for any night and the importance of keeping me on schedule and on message. John and I had complete trust in them. John and I had agreed that it was important for me to have someone like Dan or Noel every night, as I had a tendency to stay too long at doors, to get involved in debates or even lose the head if things went wrong. These weren't yes-men and they had the ability to read me and what was happening on the ground.

John then had the responsibility of determining the composition of the teams, and, like many things, it's easier said than done. When you go out with a group of people the individuals you have around you create an impression, and this is what people can use to judge you. Where possible we tried to rotate people around so that everyone got an opportunity to canvass with the candidate and with the second or other teams. We also tried to balance the groups in terms of age, sex and political experience. Nothing will turn off a new canvasser more than being the only novice in a group of wise old heads or being flung into the deep with no support. Thankfully I didn't have to organise these groups. This was one of the many headaches I was only too ready to hand off to my strategy team.

There were always things to manage and arrange on the nights out in canvassing. There were friendships, interpersonal difficulties, blossoming relationships and jealousy. All these dynamics had to be managed. Whenever possible I'd ask the lads to go in canvass pairs, but sometimes these pairings would go horribly wrong, with people threatening to go home or not come again if they were paired with a particular person. There were also some canvassers who would only canvass with me, the candidate, and then there were others who would only canvass with the second or third team, because I was a hindrance to them. Paul O'Connor in particular was a guy who would hate canvassing with me, as one of the rules of canvassing with the candidate is that you can't go too far ahead of him or her. Paul is a good canvasser and is a fitness fanatic. The thought of standing waiting for me while I was at a door for twenty minutes used to drive him mad.

John and I finish our last conversation: 'Kid, you were some candidate. Thanks for a rollercoaster of a ride. It was some experience. Get some rest, turn off mobile, don't answer phone to anyone, only me, and pull out the TV and radio. Now get some rest and enjoy a peaceful morning,' as he smiles.

Friday 25 May

Count.

RTE exit poll. Depressing news on 'Morning Ireland' as the exit poll shows we would see an increase of around 4 per cent whilst Fianna Fáil would win almost exactly the same share of the vote as in 2002.

Poor Dan Boyle was in a no-win situation and was dumbfounded at the exit polls. 'FF in pole position and the figure being quoted is at the lower end of our expectations and we will depend on transfers to increase our seat targets...' How prophetic his words were when he said, 'Fears support for Green Party was expressed in high preferences rather than number 1 preferences...'

So from 7:00 on count day we knew that Bertie and FF have won three in a row.

Sometimes it seems that life is just a string of missed opportunities. You look back on years—decades—past and wonder why: what should I or we have done different.

The exit poll in 1997 was accurate, but it's going be a long, long day.

Tallies are encouraging as, drip by drip, information gets out. By now I have ignored all John's advice and am listening to and watching TV and radio.

We are in with a shout, but it's close.

The day of the count for me is the most exciting of the election. You will never see any electioneer getting more emotive than they would on the day of the count. It is, however, the one day when you will empathise with the opposition when one might lose their seat. Well, to an extent anyhow. It's heartbreaking when you don't win a seat after all the hard work you put in and when you are passionate about politics and you believe in the person you are campaigning for; it's hard not to take things personally.

Experience in politics allowed me not to take it personally. I learned from this experience that no matter who you are, the electorate will invariably look after number 1. So unless you have seven thousand best friends living in the constituency you can expect that the majority of people who vote for you are voting for you for reasons other than anything personal. Indeed a lot of voters who voted number 1 for me would probably have liked to give their number 1 vote to a number of candidates, and vice versa, but can only give it to one person.

Therefore, people's mood on the day can have a material effect on the outcome. If the election was two days later, who knows? We might have had a tighter election. Not that it could get much tighter! A few hundred votes around the country could well have seen Fine Gael and Labour with three more seats, leaving Fianna Fáil with three less, hence a strong change to a Fine Gael-Labour-Green government.

I miss arriving at the count at 9 a.m. I loved overlooking the tallies, but the buzz of actually doing the tallies is one you can't describe. It involves sitting over a box while the votes are emptied out of it. As they are placed in a bundle the tallyman must check each ballot paper to see who received the number 1 vote and mark it off on their card. The results of all the boxes are accumulated, and before the votes are formally counted we have a fair idea of the amount of number 1 votes. It's not always very accurate, as we were to find out later in the day.

Noel's task on the day was to tally the transfers. I had asked a few people who had been on the campaign with us to help me out on this so that we could just get an idea of what to expect after the first count. He found that I was getting a fair share of transfers from the independent candidates. What we did notice, however, was that the other two Fine Gael candidates, Simon Coveney and Deirdre Clune, were transferring to each other, but not to me. This meant that if I was ahead of either of these candidates there was a danger of only one seat for Fine Gael.

From early on we also noticed that two candidates who we thought would transfer better to me didn't, two candidates in my local ward, Henry Cremin and John Dennehy. Dennehy was giving his fair share to me, but I thought there would be a higher percentage. We are opposing parties, and it seemed that this time around there was a large portion of the electorate voting for the party as opposed to the candidate. If Dennehy was to be eliminated before me, I was confident that I would be elected, given that the other two Fianna Fáil candidates were safe.

The main parties work together on the tallies. It's easier that way, and it takes less resources to give the estimate of votes. A few people from among the parties were working on accumulating the totals. A tally spreadsheet was done up before the count, which was a very detailed sheet and gave a breakdown of every candidate's vote by ballot box. This then fed into a summary spreadsheet, from which we took our figures throughout the day.

The person who was organising the tally, however, was very protective of the results on the spreadsheet, for reasons best known to himself. This meant we only received an up-to-date spreadsheet of what was going on every hour or so. I didn't see any reason for this. In truth, it was ridiculous.

Cork North-Central had a screen and a projector, so that everybody could see the up-to-date tallies. Only the select few managed to get the results every hour on our side of the boundary.

When the final tallies were issued by our man, he again only gave them to the select few. I managed to get the spreadsheet copied to my memory stick so that I could analyse the numbers. One thing that came of this tally was that Deirdre Clune was getting a seat, and that she had done particularly well in my base, the

South-West Ward ... Impossible! How can it be that she can get almost the same number of votes in my own ward? John Buttimer questioned our tally officer about it straight away and was blown off by him, saying that the numbers were final and that was that.

Noel and I decided to head back to Dino's house to go over the numbers. Clune was 1,700 votes ahead of us, but Coveney was only 500 ahead of us according to the tallies. Noel painstakingly went through each ballot box figure, as we knew there had to be a mistake. We found it. Clune's votes in one of the boxes had been overstated by 1,300. Game on, I thought! The gap is narrowed to 400 votes; we can do it on transfers ... Wait, are we beating Dennehy? Only by 300 votes. It was going to be tight, as he would pass us out on transfers from Martin's surplus.

I can't begin to imagine how Deirdre Clune must have felt after she found out her tally was overstated by 1,300 votes. She must have thought she was safe but now had a battle on her hands. Her father-in-law had died that morning also, which was obviously a huge blow for the family.

We were on a high for about fifteen minutes after discovering the real final tallies. But the more we analysed the numbers, the more we realised that it might be out of our reach. I was still hopeful, but I was getting more into reality mode. I was preparing for the worst. I knew we were too far behind.

It's about 7 p.m., and the official first count is to be called. Tim Healy, the returning officer, takes to the podium. The results are as follows:

   Dan Boyle: 4,945
   Jerry Buttimer: 5,180
   Deirdre Clune: 5,739
   Simon Coveney: 5,863
   Henry Cremin: 3,020
   John Dennehy: 5,062
   Maurice Fitzgerald: 30
   Gerard Linehan: 155
   Ciarán Lynch: 5,466
   Mícheál Martin: 11,226
   Michael McGrath: 9,866
   John Minihan: 1,596
   Ted Neville: 804
   Morgan Stack: 116

It was over! I knew it immediately and filled up with emotion. The tallies were wrong, and we were 600 votes behind Clune and only 100 ahead of Dennehy. There was no going back.

I arrive at City Hall and I'm feeling good; I actually am resigned to being defeated and decide that this is no place to hide. Watching the tallies, it's clear that the votes are not coming and that I am going to be eliminated.

Tim Healy is the returning officer, and he walks over to tell me after this count he's going to have to eliminate me. He smiles and says, 'You gave it a good shot, you gave them a run for their money, but I'm sorry, the next process is your elimination. It's almost time.'

So Team Buttimer gathers in the centre of the area where our count is going on. I pick a spot on the roof just above Tim Healy and stare at it. Dad, as always a tower of strength, is alongside me, as are John, William and Mary and the crew.

I think of Mum and her great support and of course her two famous sentences, 'The ballot box is a great leveller'; 'Run and see who your friends are.'

Nothing prepares you for when the returning officer steps to the podium and decrees: 'I now propose to eliminate Mr Buttimer, being the lowest-lying candidate, and distribute his papers.'

With those lines the campaign is over; there is no way back. The people have decided and you're out on this occasion. The applause means nothing; we lost. It doesn't help that we brought an extra 9 per cent to FG or that we won an extra seat. No, strangely, I felt like I let down Enda and the gang by not winning.

The name of the game is winning; there is no prize in politics for coming second.

Sitting in the City Hall, feeling down I have to admit, a young girl asks if I'm disappointed. 'My Mam voted for you, and my class liked your smile.'

I am not bitter, just fiercely competitive, and had a desire to win. I am a FG person. What hurt most was a comment passed by someone who should have known better: 'Well, let's see if Buttimer does the job he was put there for and delivers the votes.'

In other words, would we transfer to the other two FG candidates? I knew we would and didn't even bother analysing the transfers. Others in the party were doubtful. In my mind, anybody who questioned our loyalty to the party was not a party person themselves. People who questioned it were not loyal to the party but rather to a particular candidate. As it happens 65% of my votes went back to Clune and Coveney with more going to Clune as she was also a city-based candidate. This was to be expected. They both got elected, which was a consolation for us.

What was going on right at the end of the campaign? The move to FF ... Where did we lose it? If I had said anything at a few doors where I had disagreements, would the result be different now? Or is this the way things were supposed to end up, the dynasties to continue winning?

Part of the torture is not knowing what could have been. It's a shame we don't get to live parallel lives. Politics and life don't allow that.

I can't say what is provoking these thoughts, other than a collection of 'possibly missed opportunities.' I think of Jim Corr, Thomas Ryan, Dino Cregan; all ran and didn't win. I now join the list.

It's back to school! Do I really hate teaching in school? So many people, society, were changing around me—so many people have changed. And, strangely, I feel like I haven't changed enough.

It's easy to get lost in thoughts about what could have or what should have been, and in doing so you neglect what is actually going on. People decide and that's it.

My motto is 'Live for the day.' We have to continue to resurface after each day. Resurface from the defeat, the mistakes, the heartache . . . even if we don't look back again. But we always look back.

John and I at 3 a.m. decide it's time for bed. As always, he has to have the last word. 'We fought a brave fight but just fell short. At least we didn't back down from them. We can hold our heads up and know that Bishopstown voted for you.'

I just turn and say emotionally, thanks, and let's see where we lost out and plan for the next one.

But we always look back.

Saturday 16 June

The Seanad campaign's reputed to be one of the toughest elections, if not the toughest, to win. It's a case of 'Discover Ireland'—a tour of the 26 counties: Fine Gael councillors, independents and others along with TDs to be visited. Seanad elections take place within ninety days of the dissolution of Dáil Éireann, and there'll be 149 of us vying for 49 seats, contesting five panels.

I've got no nomination yet, but I decide to head off. The word is positive ahead of the Fine Gael Seanad Commission. Fine Gael for this year's commission appointed Enda Kenny, Frank Flannery and Phil Hogan to nominate the inside nominees.

Like the general election, I call to Mum's grave to say hello, pray and hope for the best.

West Cork is the first destination; John O'Shea, outgoing mayor, is my first call, followed by Councillor John Collins and then on to meet the re-elected Paddy Sheehan and his wife, Frances, who are holding clinics in the Parkway Hotel. Little wonder he won the seat back.

Maura Cal McCarthy has dinner ready. Most welcome, it was bacon, cabbage and white sauce. The hospitality is great and the dinner was gorgeous.

Saturday night having dinner with friends in Amicus restaurant, it seems like an eternity. No call, no messages, only lads waiting for news. What's going on?

Sunday 17 June

Awake early and no news from the FG Seanad Commission. John and I head off for Thurles for Cork v. Waterford in the Munster SHC. As we arrive in Thurles a phone call comes through from Tom Curran, general secretary, informing me that I have received a nomination to run on the Labour panel. 'I am pleased to inform you that you have been nominated by the party that founded the state to contest the Seanad election. Your mother would have been so proud.'

How right you are Tom!

The match is disappointing, as we lose, but then it's off to Cork to attend co-option conventions in the city.

Monday 18 June

Attend funeral of a good friend.

Tipp North is our first call. Long day foraging out votes. Interesting day, as we met sociable and hospitable people. Mood within FG upbeat despite not winning power, but a lot of AGMs are taking place at this time.

Tuesday 19 June

Kerry, and the weather's wet. Again. Great reaction all day. Love going to Kerry as you head into Rathmore, passing the Cadbury factory and head in to Killarney, then on to Dingle, where the scenery is magnificent.

Today is a good day, partly because I know many of the lads for a number of years. Bobby O'Connell, the FG leader on the council, Tim Buckley, Michael O'Connor Scarteen and Séamus Cosaí Fitzgerald are all known to me, which makes it easier all round.

Wednesday 20 June

Tipperary South. It is raining. Mick Fitz's house, then the home of Father Mathew.

Major talk of lack of female minister on the radio. Do we need quotas? Do we need gender balance? Why not a woman? 'Labelling it feminist is nonsense,' Laura Casey says, and I agree with her in part about the need to have more women in politics and government. Women do have a role to play. I am delighted that Billy Kelleher and Batt O'Keeffe were appointed as two of the junior ministers.

In Tipperary the rain's incessant. The land is very wet as Liam Aherne greets me at his home. The weather's something else, hard to believe it's summer. Tony Kennedy is with me. We get lost but we have great crack in the maze of roads, trying to find a new young councillor, Jimmy O'Brien.

When we did find him he was inspirational. A new young married father willing to get involved in local politics following the death of his late father, Michael.

I leave Jimmy in good mood, not worrying about the weather, being lost or about Senate votes.

We reminisce about the late Liam Burke and we travel home having had a good day, confident we secured a number of votes.

Thursday 21 June

In Co. Wexford. Needless to say, it's raining again. Larry O'Brien of Zeebrugge fame is my first port of call and from there we end up talking to great councillors—Pat Codd, Anna Fenlon and Denis Kennedy.

In Co. Wexford I learn they use wheaten straw on the thatch, oats, wheat and barley. See, a teacher's always learning.

A prophet, they say, is never accepted in his own land. Well, Pat Quigley, our constituency chairman, is a legend in Co. Wexford as a former inter-county hurler.

The warmth of the welcome is great, stories to be told, issues to be resolved, votes to be won!! But people need to be convinced.

I note there's already 500 km on the clock as we arrive back in Cork for a FG function.

Friday 22 June

The Cork players issue a statement to the *Examiner* on Semplegate as we head off to Co. Clare with Tony Spillane in tow.

It's hard not to be sorry for the lads, three great sportsmen. No consistency from Croke Park. Their unblemished record is broken, and why? Window-dressing: the authorities just want to be seen to tackle the melee. Still, not mine to wonder: my job's seeking votes in the Senate, telling my story and staying in the race.

The rain is pelting down as we drive along the road to Shannon. On 95 Live the topic is Thomond Park redevelopment. Hard to beat sport. Toyota is to be the new name of Thomond as part of the redevelopment. Outrage on the radio, but Garret FitzGerald makes a good case.

Shannon is the first port of call, where we meet Tony Mulcahy, a vibrant councillor; from then it's on to Clooney and Sonny Quinn and his wife.

A quiz question in years to come, based on what I saw in Co. Clare: how many council workers does it take to fill a pot-hole? Four council lorries on laneway, to fill one pot-hole!

Into Ennis: two Fine Gael TDs. Pat Breen and newly elected Joe Carney. Two Fine Gael men in Ennis, wonderful to see. Pat a hard-working constituency man, Joe a new man following his father.

A Polish shop in Kilrush is what strikes the eye. Amazing how far we've come.

What a view from Milltown Malbay! Oliver Greaney greets me with a smile as we chat for a while about life, politics and business.

We pass through the Cross of Spancel Hill, and summer days going to the creamery to the words of the song come to mind, then our last call in Co. Clare—to Bodyke.

Portumna, Co. Galway. Bed calls but not before I meet a work colleague whose sister is getting married. Can't go anywhere—the Senate '07 bandwagon has us moving west for the next week.

Saturday 23 June

Co. Galway. Fidelma Healy-Eames is a candidate, so it's nice to take my time.

Is it ever going to stop raining?

We leave Portumna determined not to be upset by the rain. Another day on the voyage, more councillors to be met, chatted to and hopefully crack.

Paul Connaughton TD makes us feel welcome. Thirty years' unblemished service. A record of service, constituency work done well. In many ways not the glamour man of Fine Gael but one that aspiring politicians should look up to. He works hard to serve the people and enjoys it.

Salthill's buzzing in readiness for the air show. No reluctance by the locals to talk about the water crisis. I'm taken by the number of tourists in the city. A navy ship is in the water as the helicopter overhead practises manoeuvres ahead of the air show.

Satnav not a great help to us as we battle with townlands not registering in the system. Hard to believe that Senate '07 has us all empowered with the most up-to-date technology. Mobile, satellite navigation, e-mail and more powerful cars.

On to Galway, Salthill and Newcastle. Taxi driver from Windy City in Galway giving us directions. There is a sense of a changing Ireland as our new immigrants make home here, and the appointment of a Minister for Immigrant Affairs is welcome.

Co. Mayo, the home of Enda, is our next county. Planning in rural Ireland has become a major issue, in the increasing work load of local county councillors. Striking a balance is not easy, but something can't be right when councillors are angry and frustrated when decisions go against them. Something has to change.

We roll into Kiltimagh at 10:30 p.m. Tired, hungry but content at our day. Not sure if we got votes but pleased that we had good conversations. The Bernard Dunne fight is on TV. Exciting that professional boxing is on the move, and it's good that Dunne is victorious.

Sunday 24 June

Early morning in Kiltimagh. Sun shines! Mark the calendar. Tony and I are happy.

Rolling out into Swinford, wondering what time should I call Councillor Joe Mellet at. Is it too early on a Sunday? Take the phone and call, so I do. Wake Joe? Oh, no, he's been up until 4 a.m. That's the risk one takes. Tony shouts, 'Told you it's too early.'

In fairness to Joe, he was very understanding.

New Labour Prime Minister Gordon Brown takes over as we drive through Co. Mayo. Hard to believe ten years of Labour government in Britain matched by ten years of Bertie Ahern in Ireland.

The task facing Fine Gael is not impossible; winning power is achievable provided we stay focused, united amongst ourselves and attract more young people into politics.

Lunch in Travellers' Friend is a jolly one, where we meet Senator Paddy Burke, Councillors Pat McKenna and John Keenan and fellow Senate hopeful Councillor Joe Reilly. The banter is good and the slagging is intense.

View coming into Westport is special, not to mention the village of Gweesalia (Gaoth Sáile, 'Salty Sea Inlet'), where Gerry Coyle lives.

I learn that one mile outside the village there are three houses that have the distinction of being called 'TDS' Row' locally. Henry Coyle, Pat Lindsay and

Paddy O'Toole were in fact neighbours, and Henry's son, Gerry Coyle, is keeping the 'flag flying' on this particular course

On to Sligo . . .

Monday 25 June

Monday morning. Lost sight of date, day and almost time. The Glasshouse Hotel in Sligo is one we will never forget. The carpet alone is worth going to see, believe me.

'Liveline': It's all about Bev! What a show! RTE licence fee equivalent to 10,000 people, a town approx. the size of Bray, would be left off if RTE collected all the outstanding moneys. The listeners are incensed but corporate RTE felt they had to make a settlement. I wonder who wins.

Donegal. Presentation to J. J. Reid, Bernard McGuinan for decades of services. I was happy to be there with them. When you see two outstanding servants of the party clocking up forty years of unrivalled service, it's hard not to be emotional. In Cork Jim Corr has served since the early 1970s.

Lunch with Joe McHugh in Letterkenny is a tonic. He is, in one word, a 'legend'. They all love him and he in turn has a word for everybody. In the restaurant he is inundated with people. He takes time to chat, to share a joke and is interested in the constituents.

Scenery to Gaoth Dobhair is breathtaking as we reach Dinny McGinley TD. 'A better route is available,' calls out the Satnav. 'Would you like to continue?' chimes in the Satnav system.

'Recalculating', she cries as we take a wrong turn, with both Tony and I ready to throw her out the window. It's a feature of the campaign, trying to beat the Satnav.

Missed the vote for Lord Mayor tonight in Cork as Councillor Donal Counihan assumes the office of Lord Mayor. Michael Aherne had a great year as Lord Mayor, as did his wife, Eileen, as Lady Mayoress. I make two phone calls and wish them both well.

Tony chimes in: 'If you win this you will never be Lord Mayor.'

Tuesday 26 June

The odyssey continues. Bord Fáilte or Tourism Ireland should bring all Senate candidates together as a focus group to discuss the quality of hotels, B and Bs. Tourism opportunities are plentiful, and on my tour of Ireland I notice that our service industry has become dominated by new immigrants, so that the old Irish welcome is missing in many places.

Lovely Leitrim, the only county without a TD, is our destination today. Showery and buzzing with summer as farmers busily cut the silage.

I'm impressed with the county: it's rugged, with shaggy brown hills and lofty mountains, and with deep valleys. I was struck by the beautiful lakes of Lough Gill, Lough Allen, Lough Garadice, Lough Glenade, Lough Rynn, Lough Macnean.

Good reaction from the councillors. I enjoyed the visit to Damien Brennan, a school principal who is a walking one. Out on yard duty when I call, his calm demeanour strikes me. As the kids scurry in and out he keeps a watchful eye yet at the same time has a quiet word with me.

Michael Ring in the Dáil engaging with the Ceann Comhairle, John O'Donoghue, energises councillors!

Wednesday 27 June

Heading to Sligo and Roscommon.

Getting lost trying to find Charlie Hopkins has to be one of the events of the campaign. Despite his best directions we still get lost.

>Me: 'Hello. I'm looking for Charlie Hopkins.'
>Local 1: 'You are?'
>Me: 'I am.'
>Local 2: 'Would you be one of those Senate bucks?'
>Me: 'I am.'
>Local 2: 'I see. He's living over the road about a mile yonder by Arigna.'

Local 3:	'You're from Cork city? I was there once to collect a bull. He was a good one.'
Me:	'I am, and I'm happy that the bull worked.'
Mother:	'Is there good shopping in Cork?'
Me:	'There is, good variety.'
Local:	'Aye. I'm sorry for you, but I'm not sure whether it's because you're on the Senate campaign, whether you're lost, whether you're from Cork, or because you're a Blueshirt.'

I'm not sure either, but I'm happy to reach Charlie Hopkins's house a full hour later . . .

Kitty Duignan puts us up and we tuck in to homemade apple tart. Content and ready for bed.

Thursday 28 June

A wet start to the day in Co. Roscommon. Immense amount of work being carried out in the county by Fine Gael county councillors and by all party members is noticeable as we listen to the stories.

Freddie Eynsford-Hill, *My Fair Lady,* 'On the Street Where You Live,' is playing on the radio; seems very, very appropriate. I have to admit getting lost is a part of the Senate campaign. We did it in style despite assistance of maps, Satnav and a route planner of councillors. Trying to find one of our councillors, we pull in to another farmyard in Newtown Cashel, Co. Longford, where a number of middle-aged men are killing time because of the rain. 'Department of Agriculture farm inspection team,' I call out.

'Away with you up the fields, and mind the bull, and don't forget to close the gate.'

They smile as I explain my plight. Unsympathetic, they give directions and wish me well. There he goes, they call out, another guy trying to get on the gravy train; it must be some gravy, I smile, and say, Aye, lads, give us a break, I'm only a poor teacher.

What they say next is unrepeatable. Smiling, we leave.

Ballymahon mart is my next destination. The mart, once the great institution, heart of rural Ireland, is still strong here.

Looking for my target, I ask an inspecting farmer has he seen my man; he replies, 'You'd be on the Senate campaign.'

Smiling, I say, 'I am. How did you know?'

'Well, very few farmers come to the mart in a pair of wellingtons and a suit pants, looking like a tailor's dummy.'

Stories of youthful days in Millstreet mart come to mind, but as I listen I feel a little like your man on the radio, Paddy O'Gorman, listening to farmers complaining about the prices of cattle.

The quest for Senate votes is enjoyable, apart from getting lost. The Vincent Browne show talked about an elite group picking the forty-three seats. I agree with councillors having a role in the election of the Seanad. From speaking to councillors, they take the task seriously as they select their chosen candidate. I just hope I'm one of them.

Friday 29 June

Another day. Another vote. Another town; today it's Cavan.

Today's story of the campaign has to do with our hotel. My story begins as I leave it late to book and eventually at 10:30 get a hotel room in Virginia.

Arriving at the hotel, we sign in and set off for our rooms.

I leave my door slightly ajar, and suddenly the night air is punctured by Tony's loud shout from the adjoining room. Running out onto the corridor I look at Tony, expecting him to be doubled over in agony. Instead he is at the door in a row with an American couple.

Tony opens his door to discover an American gentleman in his bed, about to be accompanied by his wife. 'What are you doing in my room?' asks Tony. 'And you can leave the dressing-gown on,' he informs the wife.

We met fellow-candidate Paul Coughlan, RTE film crew, Barry Donnlellan and FF Senate hopeful Mark Daly. A late night is had as we head to bed, tired but content.

End of day. Hard to gauge reaction. It's all of us together yet alone. Senate campaign does that. You trek around the country as an individual yet part of an organisation.

One gets the feeling that with its different strands the Fine Gael public representative is proud to be under the Fine Gael church. A church with one body, different parts but committed to its leader and organisation.

Saturday 30 June

Co. Monaghan on tour. 'O stony grey soil of Monaghan,' and so on. Met my good friend Councillor Owen Brannigan as we set off in quest of more votes. The Senate campaign is thoroughly enjoyable. I like meeting people and love listening to stories and tales of life as a councillor.

Councillor Hughie McElvaney interrogates me and asks me why he should vote for me. In his unique way he says, 'Now, Jerry, why should I vote for you, cause when you get into the Seanad you won't give two fucks about Hughie, now will you?'

It felt a bit like being on 'Mastermind' as he threw question after question at me, telling me to slow down, that I was like an old threshing machine he once owned, spitting out one or two words at a time. I think it was the speed of my Cork accent which confused Hughie.

We enjoy the crack, and when Hughie asks Owen Brannigan and me do we want tea, I'm relieved.

Carlingford is our next destination. Dad went to school there, but the drive into Carlingford is something special, as it nestles between Slieve Foy, Carlingford Lough and the Mourne Mountains. The drive into Carlingford is lovely.

Leaving Jim Darcy's house in Blackrock, we drive to Cork—a long day, a long week since we left Cork. But one full of happiness, votes garnered and a fresh approach to Irish life appreciated.

Sunday 1 July

Munster football final day as we head to Co. Waterford to canvass more votes. It's strange not being in Killarney, my first match missed in a long time. Waterford is frustrating, as many councillors are out, on holidays and committed to Maurice Cummins.

I don't mind the latter, as you would expect people from one's home county to support the local guy.

Councillor John Carey is our tour guide for the day, and all is going dandy until we try to find Liam Brasil's house, somewhere outside Leamybrien. We wind up on the side of a hill with grass growing in the middle of the narrow road.

Monday 2 July

Ah, God bless Mrs Abbey and her coffee cake; it was sweet and most welcome. John in the car for an hour is wondering what we were doing. As I tell him about the cake and the tea he starts to drool. He's badly in need of food as we set off for Carlow. Just two weeks to go until polling will commence.

Passing through Glenroe, the song 'The Byroad to Glenroe' comes to mind.

Wicklow is our final call and a stop-off with Irene Winters, a town councillor.

Tuesday 3 July

Another day, another vote to be won. John and I are full of life and mischief as we hit west Wicklow and Co. Laois.

Descending from the Wicklow Gap into Glendalough, where the monastic settlement was founded in the sixth century by the hermit Saint Kevin. The drive is spectacular and, in the words of Wicklow Tourism, 'the towering peaks of the Wicklow Mountains, covered in forests, are reflected in the two lakes that give the valley its name—"the glen of two lakes".' It really is a beautiful and special place.

The event of the day is John missing his bus to Cork and having to drive to Dublin with me. He's not impressed.

Wednesday 4 July

Spent the day in the Dáil and the afternoon on Dublin's north side.

Thursday 5 July

Meath and Louth. All becoming a bit of a blur.

Friday 6 July

6,716 km on the clock as we start. Time means nothing. Focus on winning votes.

Saturday 7 July

Limerick, and 7,500 km on the clock. I'm here seeking transfers. All day on road as we arrive in Limerick. Dan's encyclopaedic knowledge of the geography is a help.

Sunday 8 July

Kilkenny is the county today. It's the Munster hurling final, Limerick v. Waterford. Impressions of day are of hospitable people and many out. There is something about Ireland and of rural life in the summertime especially. Restores the faith.

Monday 9 July

Rains incessantly as I head to Limerick with Noel Ranahan. As expected, it's all the locals here and I am happy to court number 2s. Have to return to Cork for a city council tonight for a vote on the Gaelscoil. Can't forget the local issues.

Tuesday 10 July

Dublin and Kildare are my targets today. Traffic in Naas is incredible as I take off on a tour of Ireland via Punchestown. I end up going the wrong way, as I reach Balitinglass and then into Tallaght. So much for my sense of direction.

Get to Dublin, stopping off in Karen Warren's house for a cup of tea.

Wednesday 11 July

Up early, out to Kildare, Maynooth—my alma mater—and then on to Longford to meet some of the councillors I missed when I was there last.

Barley Harbour is one of the nicest places I found, and its description does not do it justice. 'Just across from Quaker Island on Lough Ree lies the secluded Barley Harbour.' It and the adjoining Elfeet Bay is one of the most attractive and scenic locations on Lough Ree.

New councillor Michael Kinsella and I were due to meet in Tullamore but fate decreed that I drive to his house. And from there I met two others in Tinahely and in Enniscorthy. On way home I felt tired and was tempted to stop and book a hotel room.

Listening to radio, or so I thought, I heard the rumble strips and awake to the side of the ditch. I wasn't sure if people ever fell asleep driving but it was a scary moment as I stopped, got out, walked around for a while, and then drove back to Cork.

Thursday 12 July

Tipp North and a visit to the Premier County. Tony Kennedy helps pass time as we canvass.

Friday 13 July

Day off.

Saturday 14 July

Galway to meet a number of councillors that I missed on my first trip. Enjoyable meeting with Pádraig Connelly and Brian Walsh. William manages to skirt the car successfully around the roundabouts and kerbs of Galway. Pádraig Connelly was to be my last call, but on the way home I get a call from my friend Dino Cregan asking me to go back to Kerry to meet the lads I missed.

Meet Gerry Breen and his wife, Maeve, in Galway. Good to meet them, but it's a long, long day as the car rolls in home. Just one more day to go.

It's hard to imagine that the Seanad odyssey is about to close. I have to say I enjoyed the tour of Ireland, sitting in houses drinking tea, chatting, meeting people in their own environment. I am amazed at the hospitality, the warmth of the welcome and the degree to which councillors and their families go to meet us.

The FG tent is a broad one, as I wrote earlier, but under the canvas there's fierce pride, steely resolve to represent people, and a great desire to contribute.

Sunday 15 July

Last day of canvass is in Co. Kerry with former star John Egan. From tomorrow councillors will start to vote, and there's no more that can be done. Kerry is my final day. It's a long day as the car rolls in home. Just one more day to go.

Michael Gleeson is a former Kerry great who lives just outside Killarney. Written on grey slate, 'Senate candidates, Councillor Michael Gleeson,' with an arrow; one follows the arrow, then one is met with another sign: 'You have reached the end of the trail. Deposit material here.' Only in my case the sign read, 'I have already voted.'

We stop off in Killorglin, the home of Puck Fair. The fair is one of Ireland's oldest and longest celebrated and is held every year on 10, 11 and 12 August. Every year people go up into the mountains to catch a wild goat. The unsuspecting goat is brought back to the town and a young person crowns the goat 'King Puck'. The goat is then put onto a platform high above the middle of the town.

It's also home to Laune Rangers GAA Club. Off to Ballylongford to meet Tim Buckley and Liam Purtill and then back to Listowel for tea with Frank Quilter. Frank is some operator.

Last call is Rathmore, and we end up in Cahill's of Rathmore with Tom Sheehan.

I decide not to call or to text for fear of annoying people. I wonder am I right, but that's it.

Monday 16 July

Count day dawns
John, Dad and I set off for Dublin. Tension is high. Where does it all end? Defeat means a return to school; victory and I become a full-time politician. The intricacies of the Senate system mean that we had no idea of the exact time of our count. The day is punctuated with warm sunshine as we sit on the benches on the plinth of Leinster House.

The count for the agriculture panel is going on, and Councillor Aileen Pyne sitting at her desk is crunching out the numbers. It becomes clear that Paul Bradford, Paddy Burke and John Paul Phelan are going to win FG seats but the final seat is on a cliff edge between Maria Byrne and Eugene Baker.

Sinn Féin has made history by winning a seat in the Seanad for the first time as Pearse Doherty, who failed to win a Dáil seat at the general election, secured a seat on the agriculture panel. The alliance between Labour and SF here perhaps demonstrates the need for new alliances in Irish politics.

As the afternoon slips into evening, Eugene Regan wins the last seat for FG on the agriculture panel.

Then it's show time; there's no hiding now. No home, no chance of opting out. The 12,000 km I travelled, over 26 counties, seeking votes or pledges of support from councillors and TDs is about to be revealed.

The count takes place in the middle of the members' restaurant under the watchful eye of Deirdre Lane, the Clerk of the Seanad. The votes are sorted and counted into parcels and distributed. Tables surround the room, and each candidate has a place name.

What seems like an eternity, the men and women of the Seanad count drop votes onto your designated space. John and Dan are tallying the votes. Standing alongside me, Dad and Eileen Murphy are doing a running count. I just can't count, too nervous worrying about how the other FG candidates are doing, seeking a peek at the voting papers of those around me. I have no clue. Councillor Kevin Murphy encourages me.

How am I doing? Have I enough votes? Will I be caught by the inside-outside rule? The 61 becomes 61,000, and from first-count tallies I'm told I'm safe and that I will follow in the footsteps of my good friend Dino Cregan in winning a Senate seat.

The counts continue, with votes being transferred. Inching my way to the line, I was conscious of the supreme efforts of the defeated candidates. Their sense of disappointment was tangible and the tightness of voting illustrates the fragility of the Seanad system.

On count 20, following the elimination of Pat Donovan, Deidre Lane moved to the microphone and declared that I was elected to Seanad Éireann.